"As an empty nester, I laughed, cried, reflected and rejoiced as I read Dan Schaeffer's latest book. The privilege and impact of good parenting were brought to life by important truths illustratated with candid observations about his own parenting. I recommend this book to all who desire to be the parents God has intended them to be."

Dr. William J. Hamel, President
Evangelical Free Church of America

# WHY I WEAR A PLASTIC DINOSAUR

# Why I Wear a Plastic Dinosaur

### A CALL FOR DADS TO SEIZE THE MOMENT

Dan Schaeffer

## HORIZON BOOKS

A DIVISION OF CHRISTIAN PUBLICATIONS, INC.
CAMP HILL, PENNSYLVANIA

# HORIZON BOOKS

A DIVISION OF CHRISTIAN PUBLICATIONS, INC.
3825 Hartzdale Drive, Camp Hill, PA 17011
www.christianpublications.com

*Why I Wear a Plastic Dinosaur*
ISBN: 0-88659-209-0
LOC Control Number: 2001-131918

© 2002 by Dan Schaeffer

To Christi, Andrew and Katie: my inspiration. You have taught me far more than I have ever been able to teach you. I thank God for you always and pray for you daily. Thanks for overlooking my failures, mistakes and love of old black-and-white TV shows. Daddy loves you very much.

Annette, thank you for helping me become the father I want so desperately to be. And thank you from the bottom of my heart for giving me three of the most precious possessions any man could ever hope to have. Your husband loves you very much.

Heavenly Father, I thank You for teaching me so patiently what it means to be a father. You redeemed all my mistakes and allowed me to say, "Surely I have a delightful inheritance" (Psalm 16:6). Most of all, thanks for being my Dad. Your son loves You very much.

# CONTENTS

# INTRODUCTION

# have you noticed that . . .

. . . being a father is full of poignant moments? They surround us on all sides. They are found in the unexpected words of our children, in a hug we didn't foresee, in the tears in their eyes, in the moment we see our children doing what we had always prayed they would. In these moments, as varied as the colors of the rainbow, we laugh, wonder about life, cry about something we can't explain and carefully tuck these moments away in the memory galleries of our heart. We are dads.

The funny thing is that these moments are holy and special to us alone, for reasons we have difficulty explaining. They touch us, define us, move us and can change us profoundly, yet these moments are tame to the outward eye, seemingly just part of the plain, bland fabric of fatherhood.

But though these moments envelop us, we too often miss them, for they are shy. Much of the "meaning of life" that we hear about and experience all too infrequently is made up of these tender moments. Every now and then we realize we are missing precious moments with our children. Caught up in the bustle of life and our own private ambitions, we know we need to stop and smell the roses. We love God and our families, but can feel our priorities slowly reshuffling.

To become aware of these moments of wonder, we must slow down, reflect and listen well and long. Busyness is often the thief of meaning. The tear we need to wipe away, the game we need to attend, the encouragement we need to give, the door our children bid us enter in their lives can so easily be missed.

Though these moments are free, you could no more buy them than you could buy a pleasant dream or a moving sunset. And they cannot be stolen, for their value is in your eyes and heart only.

Yet they can be shared. It is my goal in this writing to do precisely that: to ignite a latent desire for a richer and fuller experience of Christian fatherhood, to help kindle the wonder and meaning of your own experience as a divinely appointed dad. Priceless moments of fathering don't occur more in one life than another—they are only noticed more. But noticing is not a skill we are born with; it is one we have to develop. We often see much but notice little. Noticing requires waiting a little longer, thinking a little deeper, wondering a little more, hurrying a little less.

We know God has spoken in His Word, yet His truth cannot be contained only on sterile white pages. The eternal truth of God, found in our Bibles, also reverberates in His creation and is echoed in our children. It is at times silent and still, and at others loud and clear. They are the lessons of truth that cause us to stop stumbling clumsily through fatherhood and walk more carefully and thoughtfully, taking care of what we value and where we are headed. But you have to be looking for these lessons, receptive and in search of wonder amidst the usual and ordinary.

This is not a call to some kind of mystical fatherhood, but to a passionate, intimately involved fatherhood that seeks to adopt the heart of our heavenly Father. In this small collection of recorded moments, I pray your heart will be stimulated to see beyond the ordinary, beneath the routine, through the commonplace, to experience the life-changing truths of God written on unfamiliar paper.

Often some of the greatest changes in our lives are the results of these moments. In fact, that's why I have been known to wear a plastic dinosaur. . . .

# why i wear
# a plastic dinosaur

Why would a respected member of the community, a leader of hundreds—a pillar, even—shamelessly walk around with a plastic dinosaur attached to his suit?

The answer to this question began one day as I was pulling out of my driveway. I was in a hurry to run an errand when I saw my son running toward me, his little hand outstretched. I quickly rolled down the window and asked him what he wanted.

He smiled, his tender young eyes glowing with excitement. "I've got a present for you, Daddy," he said.

"Really?" I said, feigning interest, frustrated at the delay and hoping he would hurry up.

Then he held out his hand, slowly opening his fingers to reveal a five-year-old's treasure. "I found them for you, Daddy." What lay in those small hands was a white marble; a small, very old and bent metal race car; a broken rubber band and several other things I can't recall. How I wish now that I could.

"Thank you, son," I said, not meaning a word of it but making sure I sounded like I did.

"Take them, Daddy. They're for you," he gushed with pride.

"I can't right now, son. I've got to go somewhere. Why don't you go put them on top of the freezer in the garage for me?"

His smile fell, but he obediently started walking into the garage, and I drove off. From the moment I started down the street I felt remorse. This had happened before. I made a mental note that when I returned I would accept my gift with more graciousness and gratitude.

As soon as I drove back in our driveway I sought him out. "Hey, son, where are those neat toys you had for me?"

His expression was blank. "Well, I didn't think you wanted them so I gave them to Adam." Adam is a little boy who lives down the street, and I could picture him accepting these treasures with a great deal more gratitude and excitement than I had.

This hurt, but I deserved it. It hurt not simply because it highlighted my thoughtless reaction to his gesture, but because it triggered memories of another little boy I remembered.

It was his older sister's birthday, and his mother had allowed him to pick out something for her at the old five-and-dime. He agonized over that decision because he had only been given a couple dollars. He walked through the toy department again and again without success. There were many toys, but none that seemed quite right.

He wanted to get her something that she would just love! Then he spied it, sitting on the shelf, fairly shouting for attention and low enough to be seen by six-year-old eyes. It was perfect. Nothing else even compared to it. It was a beautiful round plastic bubble gum machine filled with gaily colored, chewy treasures.

What child would not be enthralled by the thought of bubble gum proprietorship? It was hard containing his enthusiasm. He wanted to show it to her almost as soon as he brought it home, but valiantly resisted the urge. The wait would only heighten her delight.

Later that evening at the birthday party attended by all her young friends, two years older than he but acting much older than that, she began to open her new gifts. With every new gift she squealed with delight.

And with each squeal, the little boy felt more apprehensive. These little girls were from wealthier families than his, families who could afford to spend far more than $2. Their gifts were expensive and shiny and talked and went potty. He began to worry as his little package seemed to grow smaller and more insignificant.

Yet he managed to remain eager to see her eyes sparkle as she opened his gift. After all, she hadn't received anything she could eat or collect pennies with. She finally finished opening all the other gifts, but still hadn't noticed his, because it had been covered over with all the other expensive wrapping papers.

He quickly pointed out her oversight. It was understandable. She was busily engaged with her friends, drinking up her role as belle of the ball, a part she seldom got to play. In retrospect he realized that was probably more meaningful to her than the gifts, but he couldn't understand that then.

She dutifully opened the gift, and he immediately saw it in her eyes: she was slightly embarrassed at it. Suddenly the beautiful bubble gum machine looked like the small, plastic, cheap toy it was. To maintain her standing among her peers she couldn't acknowledge the gift with too much enthusiasm. There was momentary silence as she deliberated her response. Then she looked at her friends, smiled knowingly at them and turned back to the little boy with a safely patronizing tone and said, "Thank you. It's just what I wanted." Several girls tried to contain their giggles, but they weren't very successful.

Quickly she returned to her next birthday game, and the little boy looked away feeling hurt and confused. That bubble gum bank had seemed so beautiful and wondrous and special in that five-and-dime, but now it suddenly seemed very small and cheap.

He slowly picked it up and walked out to the back porch of his country home and tried not to cry. His cheap little gift didn't belong with those other expensive ones; it was merely an embarrassment. The least he could do was protect her from that.

The laughing and celebrating continued inside, which seemed to increase his torment. The door soon opened and his mother appeared. "Why are you crying?" she asked. He told her as best he could.

She listened silently, then went back inside. In a few moments his sister appeared alone. He could tell by her expression that Mom had gotten her, but her remorse reminded him that she hadn't intended to be mean or hurtful. She was only eight years old and unaccustomed to the task of balancing the difficult demands of others' feelings and queen-for-a-day euphoria.

She explained kindly in her grown-up, eight-year-old way that she really did like his bubble gum toy very much. He said he understood, and he did. She was just being nice.

I thought I had forgotten that incident—I was that little boy. Now it had come full circle. A new generation was being faced with the same choice, except this new generation was

mine, flesh of my flesh, bone of my bone. This new generation must decide whether it really is the thought that counts,
and my response would play a large part in his decision.

---

### This new generation must decide whether it really is the thought that counts, and my response would play a large part in his decision.

---

Growing up we were always told that the price of a gift
wasn't important; it's the thought that counts. But that can
be so hard to believe when Daddy gushes over an expensive
new bike but ignores a primitive token of love painstakingly
created with tiny hands and huge hearts that care about him
far more deeply than the hands that assembled that expensive new bike.

Which all leads me to the daunting question I had to face
that Christmas, the Christmas that my children were given
money by their mom to buy me presents at a school "Mistletoe Mall."

Now Mistletoe Mall is a kindergarten through sixth grade
holiday emporium of gifts of the variety you can't find in just
any store. They are more like what the stores wouldn't carry if
you paid them. But they are all designed for a child's budget,
and kids love it.

So they had bought my presents and were trying very hard to
keep from telling me what they got me. Especially my son. He
would tease me with my gift. It was now under the tree, crudely
wrapped and small, but not a day went by that he didn't make
me guess what it might be.

On Christmas morning, very early, *very* early, an excited and impatient little boy thrust it at me. He insisted I open his first. He was giddy with excitement, obviously sure I would never receive a gift of this caliber again.

I excitedly opened it, and there it was, truly the most wonderful present I had ever received. But I was no longer looking at it through thirty-five-year-old eyes, jaded by promises of "newest technology" and "faster, easier and more economical," but once again through five-year-old eyes.

It was a green plastic dinosaur of the Tyrannosaurus Rex variety. It was several inches long. But my son soon pointed out its best feature. Its front claws were also clips so that you could—you guessed it!—wear it all the time.

As long as I live I will never forget his eyes as I looked at him with my plastic dinosaur. They were filled with the expectation and hopefulness and love that are found only in very young eyes.

History was repeating itself. That small blond-haired, blue-eyed face was asking me the same question I had asked years before: is it really the thought that counts? I thought of how he must have agonized in the Mistletoe Mall to find a jewel among all the assorted paraphernalia that would best communicate his five-year-old feeling of love to his daddy.

I answered his question the only way a five-year-old would understand. I put it on immediately and raved how "cool" it was and confirmed that, yes, he was right, I did "love it." For the next several weeks I went everywhere with a plastic dinosaur clipped to my lapel. Strangely, no one seemed to notice, especially when I was in the presence of my son. No one, that is, except him.

As a result I now have an impressive collection of thoughtful gifts adorning my office. There is the hardened clay face with a permanent expression of deep abiding pain frozen in place. (It was supposed to be a smile, but that clay is hard to work with.) For several weeks I had a plastic cup sailboat and a napkin and straw parachute.

> When we reward heartfelt expressions of love toward us in a lovingly crude picture, a grammatically botched message or any other way, we teach them that such gifts are good and worthwhile.

But mostly I have fun, for my son and I now speak the same language. He gives me a gift out of the depths of his heart, and I give one back—true appreciation. It costs me nothing but gives so very much.

And isn't that the way our heavenly Father loves us? Every gift He gives us is straight from His perfect heart and the only response He desires is heartfelt gratitude.

It has occurred to me that the expressions on the faces of young children giving gifts of the heart, especially at Christmas, are dramatically different than those of adults trying to buy love with expensive electronics or jewelry.

When does the thought stop counting? It is a question I have asked myself time and time again. I guess it stops counting the moment the rewards for the most precious acts we perform for each other are reduced to their strictly commercial value. It is impossible to be perfect, like our heavenly Father, to see clearly all that is in our children's hearts. But when we reward heartfelt expressions of love toward us in a lovingly crude picture, a grammatically botched message or any other way, we teach them that such gifts are good and worthwhile. We also prepare them for how, one day, they are to love their heavenly Father. The raw commercial value of my son's presents wouldn't amount to pennies, but I guarantee you that J. Paul Getty never had enough money to make me part with them.

So the next time you see someone wearing a crude paper tie, or a "cool" five-cent (removable) caterpillar tattoo that doesn't quite fit the mold of respectable adult fashion, don't bother laughing at him or somehow feeling sorry for him.

If you tell him he looks stupid, he'll just smile and say, "Maybe, but I've got a six-year-old son who thinks I'm the best thing since peanut butter, and there isn't enough money in the U.S. Treasury to lure me to take it off."

And that's why I wear a plastic dinosaur—and I know where you can pick one up.

> If you then, being evil, know how to give good gifts
> to your children, how much more shall your Father
> who is in heaven give what is good to those who ask
> Him! (Matthew 7:11, NASB)

## TAKE TIME TO REFLECT

1. Have you ever done anything embarrassing in order to please or encourage your children? What did you do, and do you think it ultimately helped or hurt them?
2. What is the most meaningful gift you ever received from either your father or mother? What made it so special? Do you still have it today?
3. Has your child ever offered you something of great value to him or her that you took lightly? What was it? If you had it to do over again, what might you do differently?

4. As a child, did you ever offer anything special to your mom or dad? What was his or her response? How did this response affect you?

5. Have you ever given your child a gift at a birthday or Christmas that had no monetary value? (Possibly something of yours, or a "Daddy Promises to . . ." coupon book, etc.)

6. Try to come up with three creative ideas for gifts to give each of your children that have no significant monetary value, but yet will still communicate your love. (If you are in a group, share your ideas with others and start a collection to use in the future).

7. Not including your salvation, what gift has God given you that you might have taken or received too lightly—never properly thanking Him for?

8. Think of a gift you could give your heavenly Father that would come straight from your heart and touch His.

9. Finish this sentence: The greatest lesson I have learned from giving my children gifts is . . .

10. Finish this sentence: The greatest lesson I have learned from the gifts my heavenly Father has given me is . . .

CHAPTER 2

# heart to heart,
# passion to passion

A number of years ago, we purchased William Bennett's *The Book of Virtues*, and one night, after reading stories on honesty to our children, I asked them to share what each of them had learned. After they shared their answers, I suggested that they ask God in their prayers to help them apply what they had learned.

But all the while, I remember thinking, *Are they getting this?* It's a question I ask a lot. Every dad struggles with this question from time to time. Often children have grown up in church and in a Christian home, learning Bible stories and verses, but still the lingering question remains: do they really understand this?

When the prayer time came, my oldest prayed a very correct prayer, logical and deductive of all the information she had heard. It had an introduction, regurgitation and a proper application. My heart sank.

Then came my second child's prayer. First came the hurried, "Thank You, Lord, for all the stuff You give us," which I'm sure he believed was the obligatory preface to all prayers. Then came the unexpected part. Slowly and thoughtfully, eyes closed and hands busy curling his hair, he started. "Lord, I pray that if a bad person steals something or lies or something, they won't go to court, but they would go to church to learn not to tell a lie. If they don't learn not to tell lies, then they can go back to court. Amen."

It is in moments like these that we can say, "They're getting it!" He understands that many of his friends lie and steal because no one has taken the time to tell them not to and/or to model integrity and honesty consistently. He knew God's Word could help them—if they'd hear it.

## Until their hearts and not just their heads are attached to the truth, I'm not succeeding.

I'm glad my eyes were already closed and the lights were out, because they suddenly became moist. This is what I pray for. All my children are bright enough and old enough to give a "right" answer to most moral questions—but that's only a small part of the battle. Until their hearts and not just their heads are attached to the truth, I'm not succeeding.

My oldest child can have a tendency at times to worship money and pursue it doggedly. This, at times, reveals itself in greed. While we had talked about this with her till we were blue in the face, all the right answers were in her head, not her heart. She always nodded numbly when we spoke about the danger of greed, and then went out, collected money by hook or crook and spent it all on herself.

One day after she had accumulated about $15, which was burning a hole in her pocket, she was invited to an amusement park by friends. When she came back she was predictably broke and bulging with sacks of stuff . . . same old story. Except, to our surprise, she began giving the stuff out. One souvenir to Andrew, Katie, Mom, even yours truly. The only one left with nothing was Christi.

Now it was our turn to be numb. Something was wrong with this picture. Had Annette lectured her before leaving? No, and neither had I.

> The ultimate goal of parenting is not
> to get our children to learn to obey,
> but to get them to want to obey.

But there was a gleam of satisfaction and joy in her eyes we'd never seen before—an excitement brought on by giving to others just for the sheer joy of watching the look on their faces and basking in their smiles. It is more blessed to give than to receive. That's what Jesus said—and it accurately reflected the heart of His heavenly Father. Christi had just taken a small step into a deeper and more meaningful life.

She had consciously used her resources to bring joy to someone else. When did that thought come to her? I don't believe for a moment she left with the idea of spending that money on anyone but Christi. I had heard her talking that morning, and that was clearly not her intent.

But somewhere, in all her shopping, looking for something to satisfy her own desires, in some way, she heard a still small voice make a suggestion she hadn't even considered: "Spend your money making someone else happy—you'll really enjoy it." Did the thought come just once or several times? Did she hear that voice before or after she had spied the much desired toy she could buy just for herself?

Whatever the case, her heart got involved in this decision, not just her head. The important thing is not simply that she did it, but that she wanted to.

No one was more surprised than we were—except maybe Christi herself. It was a tiny spark, I'll grant you, but we exclaimed our astonishment and pride in her, encouraging the spark to ignite a fire. I wish you could have seen her eyes when we expressed our delight—but then maybe you've seen this before in the eyes of your own child.

The ultimate goal of parenting is not to get our children to learn to obey, but to get them to want to obey. To see the wisdom in it for themselves and feel the delight of their heavenly Father's smile when they begin to live out the truth they have always assented to with their minds. My children aren't in need of more information; they are in need of more transformation.

It is sometimes a painfully slow process, this moving truth from their heads to their hearts. But it is absolutely essential, for you can change someone's mind without ever changing his heart, but you can't change his heart without also changing his mind. But how do we start the truth moving from their minds to their hearts in the first place? We know how to attach the truth to their minds, but are we equally adept at attaching it to their hearts?

In the introduction to Bennett's book, he writes, "It has been said that there is nothing more influential, more determinant, in a child's life than the moral power of a quiet example. For children to take morality seriously they must be in the presence of adults who take morality seriously. And with their own eyes they must see adults take morality seriously."[1]

That last phrase gives me pause. I doubt sincerely if I can ever impassion my children for something I have little passion for myself.

I have a passion for fishing, and so do my children—now. They weren't born with it; they developed it by seeing someone with their own eyes who loved to fish and stuck poles in each of their hands the moment they were old enough to hold them.

I have a passion for camping, and so do my children—now. They weren't born with it; they developed it by going camping with a mom and dad who thoroughly enjoy it, and seeing that with their own eyes. Passion, I've noticed, is more contagious than instructed.

A heart moves a heart, and a mind moves a mind, someone said once. If I've successfully passed to my children my passion for camping and fishing, it seems to me there is only one way I could fail to pass along my passion for God, and that's if it wasn't really a passion in the first place.

Maybe it's not so much their hearts I should worry about, but my own. My kids see my eyes light up when I talk about fishing or camping. They see all the work I put into preparing and all the sacrifice I'm willing to make to go. Words aren't important—they get the idea. They saw that passion bring me pleasure, they tried it themselves, and they received the same pleasure. The torch has successfully been passed.

I wonder if it can really be passed any other way. Stories and lessons can certainly contribute to this process, but they cannot alone affect it. Passion is caught—not taught.

So I've begun asking myself some questions: honest, probing, searching questions. What is my passion? Not what is my theologically precise, doctrinally accurate belief, but what really drives me? Because if all I've said is true, that's what my children will develop as passions.

Now, I have an honest passion for God's Word. It is life-changing, life-saving and life-generating. But in taking stock, I've realized that I study it in my office behind closed doors. I share it with others passionately but my children aren't there to hear it. I commit it to memory but never practice in front of them. Reading Scripture often brings tears to my eyes but they never see them. A truth of God, finally understood, fills me with more joy than fishing and camping combined. I smile, stand up and move excitedly around the room, brimming with uncontained joy—all safely hidden behind closed doors.

The "with their own eyes" part seems to be conspicuously missing in my model. Being a private person, I have a hard time letting others in on that private passion without feeling like I'm putting on a show. But it isn't a show, and maybe they need to see the tears or ask me what I'm so excited about. Maybe they need to come inside those closed doors and see what gets Daddy so excited.

That must be it. Faith is both a public and a private passion. But when I close the doors on my faith's passion, and all they are left to look at is the public display—and, well, that wouldn't be very appealing to me either.

So now the doors must open, and I must become more transparent about my most deeply held passion. It won't be a show.

In fact, I'm quite convinced that, for a while at least, it may be quite awkward.

Recently, I decided to venture out into the unknown. While praying in my office in my home, I left the door open on purpose. I began to pray and soon was oblivious to the door, until I heard the soft padding of my youngest girl's footsteps.

"Daddy?" she said softly, peering in tentatively.

"Yes, sweetheart."

"What are you doing?" she said with a quizzical look on her face. She had seen my head down and eyes closed and must have thought I had drifted off to sleep.

"I was just praying, Katie," I answered softly.

"Oh," she said, looking mildly surprised, then asked a brief question and left.

Nothing monumental, but deeply significant to me. She had probably never seen me pray anywhere but at the dinner table or her bedside. Surprisingly, it didn't hurt a bit. In fact, I enjoyed it. Slowly, I'm introducing my children to my greatest passion, and it is a novel experience for me.

But I must remember that seeing Daddy with a brown trout on the line, fighting it with an intensity and joy that must have amazed them, was what enticed them to want to have that same experience. And when they first felt the tug of the brown trout on their own lines and their hearts pounded with excitement as they fought to land a beauty, they were hooked. After that, watching Daddy fish was frustrating at best. Only fishing themselves would fulfill them now.

If I want my passion for my God to become a passion for my children, I must put that pole in their hands also. I know He will tug at their hearts, and when He does, watching Daddy's faith won't be enough anymore; they'll want their own. Heart to heart, passion to passion: there is no other way.

> For the eyes of the LORD range throughout the earth
> to strengthen those whose hearts are fully commit-
> ted to him. (2 Chronicles 16:9)

## TAKE TIME TO REFLECT

1. If you were to list your three greatest passions in life, what would they be?
2. Would you want your children to adopt any or all of your passions as their own? Why or why not?
3. Can you think of any passion in your life that your children have already adopted? If so, how does it make you feel to see them mimic your interest?
4. Are there any truths or values that you are trying to instill in your children that you seem to be hitting a roadblock with? What are they, and what have you tried so far?
5. What do you think might be causing resistance to passing on some of your passions to your children?
6. It was stated that "my children aren't in need of more information; they are in need of more transformation." Does this reflect your own feelings, or would you disagree?
7. What are some of your children's information needs?
8. Of all the spiritual truths that your children have learned, how many have they learned from you? How do you go about imparting spiritual truths to your children?
9. What do you think your children most need to see you doing spiritually? Would it be difficult to let your kids watch you doing it?

## NOTE

1. William J. Bennett, *The Book of Virtues* (New York: Simon & Schuster, 1993), p. 11.

# sand castles

amily life had been hectic: one activity after another, one job after another, one more thing to do after another. But today we were taking time off. It was a beautiful day at the beach in Southern California. I sat snuggling my feet in the warm sand under the mild sun, sitting comfortably in my chair watching the waves roll in. *This is the way life was meant to be*, I sighed to myself.

Christi, Andrew and Katie, ages thirteen, twelve and ten respectively, played on the beach. My son, now a real beach fanatic, jumped off waves and rode them with his body board, while my older daughter was off exploring somewhere. There was only my wife, Annette, and myself, and then my youngest, Katie. She wandered toward me with that "I'm bored" look of a young child who has no one to enjoy the beach with.

She asked sweetly, beseechingly, "Dad, could you help me build a sand castle?"

Predictably, I said what any red-blooded dad would say in such a situation. "Not now, honey, I'm resting. Why don't you just go play with . . ."

23

But she would not be so easily deterred. She used the one argument that fathers, at least this father, isn't good at rebutting. "But Dad, you made sand castles with Christi and Andrew when they were little." Ouch!

It's true. It seems that with the first child parents shower attention galore upon them, doting on their every glance, cry, step and accomplishment. When they want to do something we do it, because it is new for us as well as for them. They've never played with blocks before, but neither have we—at least not with our own child. It's all new for us, and we love it. It's what we dreamed of doing when we became parents.

How often had I cajoled Christi and Andrew, Katie's older siblings, into building sand castles? I would never have even dreamed of going to the beach without first making sure I had the requisite buckets, shovels and various sand molds. But slowly, I'm not sure when, it became more common, and I became less passionate about it. We love each child just as deeply as the others, but it's true that frequently the later children receive a rather diluted activity level from us dads. It is never intentional, which is why it is so easy to miss. While I hate to admit it, a "been there, done that" attitude had weaseled into my life.

And maybe it's just me, but with the increased activity of two older children, my energy seemed to be depleted. The plain truth is that I didn't want to get up off my soft seat and play with my youngest daughter. It's not something I'm very proud to admit, but it's the truth. I wanted to veg, and she was aware of it. But her words reminded me that she wanted the same attention the older two had gotten. She wanted to be able to say that Dad had made a sand castle with her too. I was a part of my daughter's memory scrapbook, and she was collecting pictures. She wanted one of me making sand castles with her.

Shaking my head and grinning, I said, "Oh, all right, let's make a sand castle." Her eyes lit up as if I had just offered to go shopping for clothes with her, and we proceeded to make a sand castle. Soon my son joined in, being the engineer of the family, and Mom came over and began to take part. While my son and wife tried to create a deep enough moat to keep the rising tide off our castle, Katie and I made the walls, parapets, flags, stairs and anything else we could imagine. All modesty aside, we had a pretty good sand castle going. It was fun again, and I soon forgot my laziness and added to my own memory gallery.

But as nature would have it, the rising waves began to lap up closer and closer to our castle, breaching our sand walls and filling our moat. While we tried desperately to stave it off, it was inevitable. We were able to admire our castle for a good ten minutes before it began to be slowly dissolved with the rising tide. No one minded, though. We had built it, and as the longevity of sand castles is a bit tenuous in the first place, none of us expected it to last too long. The fun was in the building, together. Katie was satisfied. Her smile told me she felt all was now "fair" again, and she abandoned the sand castle for some new interest.

I was left alone to sit in my chair, my feet nestled in the sand once more, my eyes drawn irresistibly toward the sand castle. It was now just a mound of wet sand, all the intricacies we had worked so hard to achieve washed away by the waves. Someone walking on the beach would never have suspected there had ever been a sand castle there. The sand would remain, but it would take another to create a new sand castle.

Then my eyes searched for my Katie, my little sand castle. I saw her playing and reflected how quickly she was growing up. Did I remember what she looked like even five years ago?

How quickly the waves of time had washed over my daughter and removed all traces of that once helpless little baby. The baby is now gone, leaving in her place a young girl turning rapidly into a young woman. It seems she was born yesterday, yet her castle is more than half finished, and there's so much more I want to add.

Years have now passed, yet when I think back upon that day at the beach, making the sand castle with Katie is all I remember about it. All those pressing details of that time in my life that so screamed for my attention are forgotten, the waves of time rapidly washing away all trace of their presence and revealing them to be much less significant than they had once seemed. What water does to sand castles, time does to life. Oh how carefully we have to choose what we do with our time! I thank God that He gave me the wisdom to see the importance of making that sand castle with Katie.

> I'm only given so much time to make sand castles with those I love, creating those memories and shared moments of togetherness that last a lifetime, before the tide comes in.

I regret all those missed opportunities when I should have made a sand castle with someone and instead nestled my feet comfortably in the sand. I'm only given so much time to make sand castles with those I love, creating those memories and shared moments of togetherness that last a lifetime, before the tide comes in. The waves of time, like the waves of the sea, allow me but a moment here and a moment there, and then all is washed away for another day. Each day is a new opportunity to make a sand castle, but someday the opportunity will be lost forever.

As I thought about this, I remembered the verse in Psalm 90 where Moses said, "So teach us to number our days, that we may present to You a heart of wisdom" (90:12, NASB). I memorized this verse years ago because I tend to live life in a hurry, always trying to reach my next goal. A good friend once told me, "Dan, you are living life like it's a race." He wasn't far off. This verse continually reminds me that time is precious, and I can only do so much with it and then it is gone. I don't get it back. As Moses said, "Soon it is gone and we fly away" (90:10, NASB) Friends, relatives, children, spouses—we're building sand castles with others all the time.

But I know I'm not alone in my struggles. I remember speaking of this one day with my sister, who with her husband was planning an expensive vacation. It was one they couldn't really afford, but one that excited their teenage boys. She admitted that the price tag was high, and they would be paying it off for quite a few months. "But," she explained, "we've only got a few years left before they're gone. This might be the last big vacation we get together."

She didn't need to say any more. There is such a thing as being penny wise but pound foolish. She and her husband were numbering their days left with their sons and realizing that either they made sand castles now or they might not get another chance. They took the vacation, and hindsight proved her right. Little could they know the importance of this decision. They took the vacation and made the memories. A little less than a year later, Brian, their eighteen-year-old son, drowned in a swimming accident and went home to be with his heavenly Father. The vacation is now paid off, but the memories it provides will last them the rest of their lives. They thank God that they built the sand castles before the tide came in.

Some things can be put off, and some things can't. It takes wisdom to know the difference. Maybe that's part of what Moses was trying to say. Everything in life is not of equal value, and time is limited, so I need to use great wisdom in where I spend those precious moments of time. Some things I can get a second shot at, and others I can't. And since there is not enough time to do everything, I have to choose so very carefully, because once I have chosen, the tide goes back out. I only have my wife, children, friends and family for so long, and then the tide will inevitably come in. I need a heart of wisdom to number my days.

Not long ago, I managed to put away some money without my wife or family knowing about it. I had a secret plan for it. But I could not help noticing that my kids were tired and worn out from school, and that my wife was running on empty. It had been a grueling few months. Without hesitation, I took $200 out of my "stash" and called the school to make arrangements for the kids to be absent. The next Monday morning, my day off, as my children sat bleary-eyed and ready to go to school, I announced in a stern voice, "Put your backpacks away!" and pointed to the closet.

They looked at me as if they hadn't heard me right. With a sly grin I opened the closet doors and motioned for them to put them away. That's when my oldest got it and shrieked with joy. She didn't know what was going on, but she knew she wasn't going to school. Soon they were all badgering me with questions as I drove them along the freeway to our secret destination.

When we finally pulled into a local theme park, there was another shriek of joy, for none of them had ever been there. We blew the wad, the whole $200, and then some. Had a blast! Irresponsible stewardship? From a certain point of view, I guess that's true, but I created a memory that I wouldn't trade for any amount. My family will always remember that day, and how fun it was, and that I took the time to plan it and take them. I hope that they will look back and remember that Dad loved to spend time with them and have fun with them. The key word is: remember. There will be something to remember.

I've built sand castles with nighttime walks with my daughter, building a go-cart with my son and having a BBQ with friends and playing family football (adults against the kids) with another family in a nearby park. None of these cost much, if anything, but they were splurges of time, and that is what we do not get back.

All our lives are nothing but sand castles, fleeting moments in which our heavenly Father allows us to respond to His repeated overtures of love. These priceless memories follow us into eternity. What God does for us, we have an opportunity to do for our children. Only one hitch—we must do it before the tide comes in. So—isn't it about time to go make some sand castles?

> So teach us to number our days, that we may present to You a heart of wisdom. (Psalm 90:12, NASB)

## TAKE TIME TO REFLECT

1. Can you name two or three things you have made together with your children? List ideas for future projects with each child who is old enough.
2. If you have more than one child, do you think your younger children have received the same intensity of involve-

ment that your first child did? Can you cite several examples? Would your spouse agree with you?

3.  Who usually initiates activity with your child—you or that child?

4.  Can you think of a project one of your children wanted you to help him or her with that you declined? If you had it to do over again, would you still decline? Why or why not?

5.  Have you ever thought of asking your older children what they did with you in the past that they enjoyed the most? What do you think they would say? Now go ask them!

6.  What is something that you've always wanted to do or somewhere you've always wanted to go with your children? List activities or places for each of your children.

7.  What holds you back from fulfilling those plans? If you knew you only had one year left with your children, would you still hold back? Why or why not?

8.  Do you ever feel as if your life is a race and if you dare to slow down, you might lose? Which of your ambitions do you feel drives this feeling? What can you do about it?

9.  "Some things can be put off, and some things can't." What are some things that you feel God may be leading you to put off till later? What things is He telling you can't be put off?

# slingshots, oak trees
# and summer mornings

It had been twenty-seven years, and I was a little rusty, but I could feel a twinge of excitement, something from long ago returning. My son and I walked under the shade of the aged oaks and sycamores, the dry, brittle leaves crunching under our feet.

We talked of slingshots. My son had a brand-new store-bought model he had saved up for and was dying to try out. I was describing the homemade slingshots I had carved from oak limbs as a boy. The sun filtered down between the twisted limbs of the trees, dappling light about on the forest floor.

My son was giddy with the excitement of a five-year-old with his first slingshot. When we finally reached a good spot, I searched for the largest sycamore leaf I could find, dry and brittle, and pressed it into the crevice of an oak for a target. After a few brief safety tips, I turned him loose to shoot, and me to remember.

It had been an identical summer morning twenty-seven years ago when a skinny toe-head with a handmade sling-shot stood in the midst of another stand of oaks and syca-mores. He was alone, but it didn't matter. It was enough just to be alive that morning.

I remembered almost everything about that morning. I had been awakened early by the sunlight streaming in through my window, beckoning me to wake and join it outside. Lying there, I listened to the morning calls of the birds. A sharp whistle rose, fell slightly, then rang clear and crisp and long. One bird called and another replied. I drank it in. I felt something at that mo-ment, something undefinable, something wholesome, good and natural. It was something I was never to forget. It was a lazy summer morning in the country.

Neglecting breakfast, I rushed outside to my front yard. We lived on the outskirts of a small country town in an old 1921 schoolhouse my father was turning into our home.

Tall, aging trees that had probably been there before the school was built surrounded it; nearby grew an apple and plum orchard. These trees were to become my playmates. I would swing on them, climb them, pick their fruit, build clubhouses in them and act out incredible adventures in them.

But not this morning. This morning I was going to learn how to shoot my slingshot, and their huge trunks were going to provide me the kind of target my modest skill demanded.

Gripping the rough wooden handle of my new weapon, I grasped a tiny stone in the leather strap, pulled back with all my might, aimed it at the trunk of one of the largest sycamores, closed my eyes and released. Almost immediately I heard the rock hit, solidly, and opened my eyes in surprise. What a shot, what a thrill, what a morning!

It was the beginning of many summer mornings with my trusty sling. I remembered the first time I placed an acorn on top of a can and with pinpoint accuracy shot it off without knocking over the can. I was never able to repeat the shot, and no one saw it but me, but I did it once.

And I remembered the time I shot a bird. I had shot at many birds and squirrels, but always missed. This time I didn't. There was the immediate thrill of exhilaration, as I saw the target fall, then the sorrow and regret as I looked at the beautiful thing lying motionless, out of place, on the ground. It might have been the one that had awakened me on so many mornings. Sadly, I picked it up and buried it, becoming a wiser boy than I had been before.

My son, who had been practicing his shooting against the oak, had finally moved close enough to the sycamore leaf to hit it. With a whack the giant brittle target cracked and crumbled, and he yelled in victory.

He then handed the slingshot to me and began exploring the forest floor. I gripped it for a moment, lost in memory. It wasn't like my old carved wooden model; it was plastic. I had wanted to carve one for my son, but he had been impatient, wanting to buy one with his own money. I had really wanted him to experience the moment exactly as I had—that's why I had brought him here. But it couldn't be.

Then something from memory flashed in my mind, and I laughed inwardly. I remembered that I had wanted a store-bought model too, when I was a boy, but I never had the money.

I picked up a nice round rock, one that wouldn't swerve in the air like a Frisbee. I hadn't forgotten everything. Aiming the rock, I gripped it in the leather sheath tightly, studied a point on the oak standing about twenty feet away, kept my eyes open and released. Instantly, quicker than I remembered, it struck about a foot lower than I was aiming, but smack dab in the middle of the trunk. I smiled.

It took me six shots before I hit the leaf target I had positioned for my son, but finally I drilled a hole right through it. I yelled for my son to look, and he glanced over and smiled, but then turned away, looking for a stick to throw.

I stood, momentarily disappointed in his reaction to my slingshot prowess, then understood. He had nothing left to prove and too much left to experience in this forest. There was bark to examine, sticks to throw, dry leaves to crumble in his fingers, red ants to observe and an old water spigot sticking out of the ground. He wasn't going to miss all this by spending all his time trying to hit a target on a tree.

> And it startled me to discover that if my targets were suddenly removed, the sun would still rise, the birds would still sing, God would still be on His throne and I would still be the eternal object of His great love.

I was suddenly very proud of him. I myself had spent too much time trying to hit targets in my life and not enough time examining bark, throwing sticks and crumbling leaves in my fingers.

How much time had I spent trying to hit all these targets, consumed and tunnel-visioned until they were accomplished? When I completed high school, I had but one target: my bachelor's degree. So I spent five years shooting at that target. Nothing interfered with that goal.

I worked forty hours a week and went to school at night, taking as full a load as my energy allowed. All my waking hours were spent studying for class. I took no long walks, gazed at few sunsets, never reflected on the purpose for it all and told myself, "It is good." I finally hit the target, but the euphoria was short-lived.

I got married, but the pace didn't slow, because now I had a new target: my master's degree. It was a three-year program and I was driven to complete it in three, regardless of the pressure that would put on my job and life in general. It would be my badge of honor, my trophy, and would prepare me for the lofty title of "pastor." It didn't matter that I now had a wife and young daughter—life was something that had to be finished, not simply enjoyed. The race again. I had to win, even if I was competing only against time, or myself.

I worked hard, studied hard, stayed up late and finally finished. I hit the target, but again the thrill was brief. It lasted one day—graduation day, to be exact.

But now I needed a new target. No time for resting or contemplating or enjoying. There were new targets to aim for. With my education finished, my career replaced that first acorn on the can, and I was just as determined to succeed.

I launched into my new career, tunnel-visioned and driven more intensely than ever before. My marriage was good and I dearly loved my daughter and new son, and I did spend time with them. But while often Daddy was physically present he was mentally off somewhere shooting at targets.

Until one day, in the midst of my target shooting, my promising career momentarily collapsed. Facing the first major crisis of my career, I felt in danger of losing my position as pastor and everything I had worked so long to achieve. It was as if God had removed the targets from my life and then asked me if I could still find happiness. I was ashamed to admit I didn't know.

I had never even faced the prospect of missing my target, much less having it removed. But it was during those days that He slowly began to reveal to me that target shooting wasn't very fulfilling, even when the target was admirable. He reminded me of every target I had ever hit, all the goals I had accomplished, and how the happiness they brought was transient. No sooner had I accomplished them than I found myself restless and ill at ease. The degrees and trophies gathered dust while I busied myself searching for new targets.

Sometimes the wisest fathers are those
who are able to learn from their children,
as well as teach them.

I remember the day I woke up and wondered what would happen if all my precious targets were permanently removed. I was lying in bed, the way I had as a boy on a summer morning, too many years ago, and I again heard the birds sing. It was a strange sound that I hadn't heard in a while, not because they weren't there, but because I had stopped listening. And it startled me to discover that if my targets were suddenly removed, the sun would still rise, the birds would still sing, God would still be on His throne and I would still be the eternal object of His great love.

Suddenly my targets seemed much less significant. The process loomed as more important than the product. I began to decompress and look and listen and rest. Vacations became more frequent and time with my family more precious.

Goals are still important to me, but now they've changed. I want to gaze at the mountains that God made to remind me that all my earthly targets pale in significance to Him. I want to stand barefoot in the banks of a rushing mountain stream with my children and remind them that with all our sophisticated technology, we are still dependent upon God for our very lives.

I want to go rafting down a beautiful meandering river with my family and spend lazy summer days teaching my son and daughters to fish. I want to experience the sheer joy of roasting marshmallows over an open campfire, gaze at His handiwork in nature and marvel together at the awesomeness of our God who could make such pleasures out of nothing. I want to spend entire evenings gazing into the beautiful eyes of my wife, dreaming dreams together, talking of our future—a future where happiness is not based on just hitting targets.

God wanted more for me than just the occasional thrill of hitting an earthly target. What my son somehow knew intuitively I had lost or forgotten somewhere in my past. Sometimes the wisest fathers are those who are able to learn from their children, as well as teach them.

Why did my heavenly Father make trees so graceful and beautiful, instead of making them all look like telephone poles? Did a sunset have to be colorful? Was there a purpose behind the myriad magnificent colors of flowers? Yes, they told me something more about the nature of the God who created them all. He delights in the beauty of His creation and beckons me to join Him. "It is good," He said, and He still means it.

Beautiful, lazy summer mornings and magnificent oak trees were my gift from Him, just another expression of His love to me. It was so simple and clear and uncomplicated a child could understand it. As I watched my son throw sticks with joyful abandon, I prayed that he would never forget, and I would always remember, that important lesson.

Soon we had to go, but even the journey back to the van was an adventure. We ran along an old rock wall, jumping over limbs that grew over it and ventured into a deep ravine, finding great enjoyment in trying to scramble out of its steep, gravely walls.

On the way back I thanked him for bringing me along. He looked at me, confusion evident on his face, this blue-eyed toe-head of mine. With his hair mussed and face flushed from the heat of the day, he said, "Daddy, you brought your own self." How could I explain that he had returned me to a place he had never been and reminded me of things I had once known? I didn't try.

However, on the drive back, we promised to come again and speak more of slingshots, oak trees and summer mornings.

> Find rest, O my soul, in God alone; my hope comes from him. (Psalm 62:5)

> Come to me, all you who are weary and burdened, and I will give you rest. Take my yoke upon you and learn from me, for I am gentle and humble in heart, and you will find rest for your souls. For my yoke is easy and my burden is light. (Matthew 11:28-30)

## TAKE TIME TO REFLECT

1. As you look back on your own childhood, what are some of your fondest memories?
2. Would you like your children to experience these same things? Why or why not?

3. When you were a child, what did you dream of being or doing when you grew up? Do you ever regret the choices you ultimately made, or are you satisfied with what you've accomplished?

4. Is there one fond memory of your childhood that you have been able to help your child experience? If so, how did he or she respond to the experience? How did this make you feel?

5. What are some targets or goals you set for yourself when you were younger? Try to list at least three or four.

6. How many of these targets have you hit? Did you experience any letdown after hitting your targets? Why?

7. What are the three most important targets you would like your own children to hit?

8. How has God changed some of your earthly goals? How did He do that?

9. Can you think of one enduring lesson that your child has unwittingly taught you? What spiritual truth can you glean from that lesson?

# CHAPTER 5

# here we raise our ebenezer

t is a rather nondescript book, tall, thin and dark blue. There is no writing on the outside, no indication of who the author is or who published the book. Of course that may be because it is a blank book. Or I should say, it *was* a blank book. Now a good deal of it has been filled in.

There is no type in this whole book, no beautiful fonts, no New Times Roman or Arial, no gold lettering or page numbers. The writing is all by hand, in different colors of pens, and done by two different authors—my wife and myself. Along with the writing are the odd, assorted mementos, pasted or taped to memorialize a special moment or event. This book is, very simply, our family Ebenezer.

It is not a photo album, nor is it a scrapbook of fun family times, both of which we have in abundance. It is our memorial to God of what He has done in the lives of our family to date. Years ago my wife and I decided it was just as important to remember what God has done for us as it is to remember who attended our daughter's third birthday party.

If the phrase "Here I raise my Ebenezer" sounds familiar, it is because you may well have sung the familiar words in the old hymn, "Come, Thou Fount." When God gave Israel victory over the Philistines, Samuel the prophet took a stone and set it up as a memorial to the occasion, calling it "Ebenezer," which meant, "the stone of help." In other words, an Ebenezer is a memorial, a signpost, a reminder of a great act of God on our behalf.

Scrapbooks are wonderful things to pass down to your children, but we decided that what we most wanted to hand down to our children was not simply pictures, but the family policy: We trust God, for He is faithful.

Ebenezers come in all shapes and forms. Some of them might not seem like much at first glance. On one of the first pages there is an entry dated July 10, 1993. It reads "Uncle Phil gave us some dugout tickets to the California Angels/New York Yankees baseball game at Anaheim stadium. Dan and Andrew went and had a great time. What a blessing and surprise! Andrew was one of the first 15,000 kids to get a free baseball bat, cup and toothbrush." Pasted right next to this entry is a ticket for Seat 2, Row C, Aisle 16.

Now this might not seem like much to you, but money was a little tight back in '93, and I was constantly looking for fun and inexpensive things to do with my son. This was an unexpected blessing that Andrew remembers. Yesterday, at age fourteen, he was swinging that tiny little miniature baseball bat. He's still got it. One day he may lose the bat or may just forget how he came by it. But one day he will be reading this book and will be reminded.

What does this tell you? Maybe not much, but it tells Andrew that there is a God who not only gives us what we need, our "daily bread," but also many other delightful gifts as well, because He loves us. These moments need markers—God loves us and delights to give good gifts to His children. So here we raised an Ebenezer.

An earlier entry is dated July 7, 1993.

> Financially we were down to our last $50. All our savings were spent on taxes and we had vacation looming before us. I had sold a number of articles to [a Christian magazine] but hadn't received any money yet. All of us started praying at every meal that God would help the people to send our checks. Yesterday (before vacation) we received a check for two articles, totaling $500. God increased our money tenfold! He answered our prayers. Great is His faithfulness.

My children were young then, but they prayed with us that God would provide for us so we could afford to go on vacation (they were highly motivated). Do you have any idea what it did to my children's faith to see those checks come in the mail before vacation? I do. But one day they may forget. One day they may be like Annette and I were, newly married, on a very tight budget, wondering how they are going to get along. I want them to be able to remember this Ebenezer. I want them to remember this stone of help.

When our children were young, we sent them to public schools. We trusted God that He would be able to guard their hearts and minds in Christ Jesus, and that they would learn to be witnesses for Him. An entry dated October 20, 1993 reads, "Christi's teachers have all been Christians. Praise God! Today, along with teaching the 'scientific' evolutionary theory, her teacher also told the class what she believed, that

God created the earth and everything in it in seven days! Who says God is dead in public schools!"

While my children never got a private Christian education, they got an excellent education on how to be a light in a non-Christian environment, lessons essential to their faith. God was so faithful to my three children. Almost all of their teachers in elementary school were wonderful Christian women. Here we raise our Ebenezer. I want my kids to learn that God is everywhere. You can't kick Him out, vote Him out or legislate Him out of anywhere. Here is a beautiful example that will remind them when they are older that God is sovereign. I am passionate about our God's tender care of us, and I want my children to share that passion.

However, not all of our entries are "happy" entries. One, dated May 1, 1994 has an obituary card pasted on the left with some writing on the right. The card was for a dear young lady who attended our church with her husband, Jeff. Her name was Becky Hess. My wife writes,

> When Becky died [two years ago] I remember praying that God would cause good to come of her tragic loss, and that we would be able to see it. God has answered both! In particular Betty Jones [not her real name], who used to be Jeff's secretary and met Becky only once, was deeply affected by Becky's death and funeral service. She points to Becky as the "thing" that made her seek out Jesus. Now she's growing spiritually in our Bible study group on Wednesdays after having accepted Christ at Harvest Crusade last summer.

Not everything in my children's lives is going to be pleasant and fun. They are going to have to go through some storms and valleys. My kids were too young to really understand much about Becky, but a few years later, when their eighteen-year-old cousin, Brian, drowned in a swimming pool, they would have to review this lesson that Mom and Dad had learned.

> My prayer is that when my kids read this Ebenezer one day—for this book will ultimately be passed down to them—they will remember that there was purpose to everything in the kingdom of God, even the death of a beloved friend or family member.

I absolutely refuse to send my children out of our home without having the necessary basic life skills. All of my children know how to pick up after themselves, do their own laundry and they will all know how to balance a checkbook, pay their bills on time and cook. My son will know how to change his oil and do basic maintenance on a car. My girls will also know how but will undoubtedly ask Andrew to do it for them. These are only a few of the basic life skills I feel are fundamental to surviving in life, and I am constantly teaching them relational skills as well.

As a pastor, I buried many people. Some of these people were only months old; some were in their nineties. Yet it always amazes me how some dads can teach their child how to rebuild a carburetor, use power tools, create a web page or manage a stock portfolio, yet never prepare them for death—their own or someone else's.

But isn't it our jobs as dads to prepare our children for their most important moments as well? My prayer is that when my kids read this Ebenezer one day—for this book will ultimately be passed down to them—they will remember that there was purpose to everything in the kingdom of God, even the death of a beloved friend or family member.

Five years later another entry, May 12, 1999, has three theater passes pasted on to the page. They represented the free passes that Brian, my eighteen-year-old nephew, had given the children only days before his tragic drowning. In this entry it reads:

> Today our dear nephew and cousin, Brian, went to be with Jesus. He knew great joy, great blessing, and great success, but more importantly, he knew Jesus as His Savior. The last time we saw Brian, he was working at Haute Cafe, trying to give us free coffee and hot chocolate. But joking and smiling the whole time, he gave us one last free admission ticket. Andrew felt we ought to put this in our book. . . . Brian will not return to us, but we will go to him. Until we see you again, Brian . . .

Do you ever think about the fact that your children will one day face the death of a loved one? We know this will happen, but we don't like to think about it. But we must. They must be ready. They must know that there is hope even through this blow in life. Not all Ebenezers are decorated with ribbons and balloons.

Another entry, dated May 4, 1994 reads,

> Katie prayed that she would be brave at the doctor's office today. She even told the nurse that she had

prayed to Jesus! When asked how she got such pretty eyes, she replied, 'God did it!' Well Katie was very brave even though the shots and pricks did make her cry. But it's OK to cry. And she knew that Jesus helped her.

When our children grow up, we want them not only to know the God we believe in, but also to know that they can indeed trust Him with everything in their lives.

As a dad, I want my children to know how much I love them. I try to show, in my own feeble way, that very thing. But that isn't my only job as a Christian dad. I want my children to know how much God loves them. While we create memory galleries through scrapbooks for them, I want them creating another memory gallery, a far more important one, featuring their heavenly Father. The most important entries are the ones that share when and how our children came to a saving faith in Jesus. There will be times when they will wonder, times of doubt, but they will always be able to see the Ebenezer. That is, if we've built one.

> When our children grow up, we want them not only to know the God we believe in, but also to know that they can indeed trust Him with everything in their lives.

There are many more entries, and most of them involve our children in some way. This is something I want to do for my kids, and you may want to try it yourself. It is only natural for every dad to want his kids to remember him in some way, hopefully a good way. There is nothing wrong with this. I desperately want my kids to look back with fondness on my memory. I want them to love me; I want them to miss me when I'm gone. I want them to know beyond a shadow of a doubt that their dad loved them. I want them to feel that they can depend on me while I'm alive for help and support in everything.

But that is only part of my job. A more important part of my job, and yours, is teaching them that they can depend on Him. There is only one perfect Dad, and we're not Him! This is my passion—that my children begin to depend on their heavenly Father for everything, just like Dad. He is faithful; they need to know this. More important than knowing how to change the oil or pay their bills, they need to know that God is faithful. More important than knowing how to cook dinner, say "no" to a salesman or avoid consumer debt, they need to know that God is faithful to care for them. More important than a strong portfolio and 401K plans is the knowledge that their heavenly Father can and should be trusted.

That is why we are raising Ebenezers in our kids' lives, recording His faithfulness in three precious blank books: Christi, Andrew and Katie. Here we raise our Ebenezer.

> Then Samuel took a stone and set it up between Mizpah and Shen. He named it Ebenezer, saying, "Thus far has the LORD helped us." (1 Samuel 7:12)

> Let this be written for a future generation, that a people not yet created may praise the LORD. (Psalm 102:18)

## TAKE TIME TO REFLECT

1. When God has done something wonderful in or for your family, do you communicate this with your children? If so, how?
2. Take some time and think of at least three special moments or events in which God showed His faithfulness to your family.
3. How do you "memorialize" special moments or events in your family's life? If you never have, are you thinking about starting?
4. Did you ever ask your children to help pray for a specific family need? What was the result? How did your children react?
5. What are some "storms or valleys" that your children have had to go through? Do you see any on the horizon for them?
6. Have you thought of how you will try to communicate God's love for your children to them? If you already are, how do you do it?
7. What are the basic skills or values about life in general that you want to instill in your kids before they leave your care? What are the basic spiritual values you want to instill in each of your children before they leave home?
8. In what special way do you think you might want to start raising Ebenezers for your family? What method do you think you might adopt?

# 6

# his lights are on, but is daddy really home?

Have you ever noticed that the ordinary moments in life seem to be the most momentous? We plan, strategize and prepare for the climactic moments we face, yet it is the unguarded, casual experiences of life that often define us. I was reminded of this several years ago as I sat in my office reading the newest edition of my favorite journal.

In the pastorate, which is often a hectic, fast-paced occupation, time is always at a premium. To stop and read—no, linger—over an article seemed almost sinful, like eating a hot fudge sundae when you're on a diet. Yet, knowing the value of this reflective time, I had just managed to become thoroughly engrossed in the article. It was at precisely that moment (please tell me why this is always the case) that my son chose to walk into my home office.

His request was simple. Could I please help him with his spelling words? He explained that all I had to do was let him write his spelling words on my back with his finger while I tried to guess what they were. Simple enough.

My next move was instinctive and reflective of the all-too-familiar pattern of busy daddies everywhere. Especially this particular daddy. I looked in his eyes with all the loving expression of a father who is always available to his children, and lied through my teeth.

"Sure, son, just go ahead. I'll turn around and you start writing on my back."

What I said and what I then proceeded to do were two different things. I never had any intention of interrupting my private luxurious moment of reading pleasure. I was just keeping up appearances.

> My son simply thought that because
> I was with him physically and answered
> his questions rationally he therefore
> had my attention.

As I turned my back to this quiet, affectionate little fellow who constantly sought me out like a lost shadow, I returned to my reading, content that I was a noble example of concerned and available fatherhood. And I would have remained in this comfortable little bubble of mine had the next few moments transpired somehow differently.

You see, my son was laboring under the conviction that he now had his daddy's undivided attention, so he began fingering the words on my back very slowly and carefully, giving me every opportunity to guess their identity. He figured, naturally, that since Daddy's lights were on, he was at home.

While I read blissfully, I could feel those tiny fingers gently tracing letters on my back. Those tiny fingers that even at the age of eight still sought to hold my own when we walked; those tiny fingers that labored for hours drawing pictures, just to hear the words, "That's great, son! You're turning into quite an artist"; those tiny fingers that penned the words on my wall, "to dady I like you Becose. your very fun and nice to me from: Andrew."

Had Daddy actually been home, he would have put the magazine down and spent five delightful minutes of fun and education with his best buddy. But he wasn't, and it wasn't the first time.

The lights were on, but Daddy wasn't home. There are probably other ways to say it, but it all comes out the same in the end. My son simply thought that because I was with him physically and answered his questions rationally he therefore had my attention.

When I turned my back, little did he know that I was tuning out, gracefully. *He'll never know*, I reasoned. *He'll think I'm really paying attention and be just as happy*. The sad part is that I've pulled it off enough times for that statement to be true.

None of this would have affected me much except for what happened next. My son dutifully and carefully traced the word on my back and then asked me what word it was.

For some reason I wasn't expecting this. I think I was hoping he'd just race through the words, say, "Thanks, Daddy" and leave. But when he finished the first word, he asked, "Do you know what it is, Daddy?"

"No, I sure don't, son." I hadn't been paying any attention, except to my journal. He wrote another one and asked again.

"Nope, you got me on that one," I mumbled distractedly.

And so it continued until he was finished. I'm ashamed to say how relieved I was. Now I could read without interruption. But apparently I hadn't been listening.

"Now it's your turn, Daddy."

"My turn for what, son?" I mumbled from the far-off pages of my magazine.

"Time for you to do me."

"What?" I said, suddenly aware I was going to be further interrupted.

"Now you are supposed to write the words on my back and I guess them." I sighed and smiled. He had me. This I couldn't do reading my journal, and I knew it.

It wouldn't take long, so I turned around, in a hurry to get done. I wish you could have seen his face. It was grinning and excited and expectant. His lights were on and he was home. I had all his attention, which I was soon going to learn in an unexpected way.

Prompted by momentary guilt, I set the article down and took the list of words. He turned around with a smile on his face as I slowly fingered out the letters to the words on his tiny back. Several times he giggled and squirmed as my fingers tickled his shoulder blades. I smiled and laughed. When I finished spelling out "there" he proudly repeated the word out loud.

Ouch! My eight-year-old son had already guessed twice as many words as I had, and we'd just begun. Well, as you've probably guessed by now, he got all but one of them. Each time he guessed the word I winced inside, each time a further reminder of how often I pretend to be present when I'm really miles away. It was over soon, and then he left.

I'd like to tell you I didn't finish the article, but I did. I just didn't enjoy it as much. God kept nagging at my heart. He was also trying to get my attention. There was something to be learned here that He didn't want me to miss, something terribly important. He gently reminded me of the catatonic state I enter when my hand grips the remote control. He reminded me how often my wife or kids try to talk to me and I am distracted and inattentive. When Daddy's lights are on, he's not always home.

> I want to have clear memories of those unguarded, unplanned moments that will become rarer and rarer as my children grow older.

One of the greatest miracles to me of my faith is the fact that at whatever time, whatever place and whatever situation I happen to be in, I can immediately turn to my heavenly Father and have His full, undivided attention. I can know that He is not only listening but also hearing me. With all the significant and catastrophic and momentous events occurring all over the world at any moment, He still waits to listen patiently and without distraction to me over the smallest, most insignificant of issues.

My heavenly Father's lights are always on, and He's always home. In the mystery of His divine nature and person, His door is always open and He's always available to any and all who seek Him out. His promise is that if I draw near to Him, He will draw near to me (James 4:8). I guess that's where my human weakness becomes apparent. For there is no guarantee that if my children give Daddy their undivided attention that Daddy will return the favor. And a favor it truly is, a temporary gift of inestimable value.

Now, I understand that I am unable to mimic my heavenly Father's flawless fatherhood perfectly, but it serves me well as a compelling model. As He is my compelling model, so I, right now, am my children's.

This is what He wanted me to see. He knew there was no malice intended—just relational laziness, but graciously God pointed out the cost of this relational laziness, and He did it with an eight-year-old boy. I was good at pretending to be attentive, God was pointing out, but was this a trait I wanted to change or pass on?

As I thought about it, I realized that ten years from now, those spelling-on-my-back moments are the ones I want to remember. I want to have clear memories of those unguarded, unplanned moments that will become rarer and rarer as my children grow older. The articles I can always come back to, and the shows are often better left unwatched in the first place.

You know, the funny thing is that I can no longer remember what that article was about, but I can still feel those tiny fingers on my back, and I can still hear the giggles as he wiggled beneath my fingers.

The point made it home, and not long after that I took a giant first step and made an amazing discovery at the same time. As my oldest daughter spoke to me about something, which I admit honestly I had little interest in, I noticed my gaze begin to shift from her to other things in the room.

Then it struck me what was occurring. Wherever my eyes go, so goes my attention. It was so simple it had eluded me. I quickly adjusted, looked her straight in the eye and actually listened. I saw a lovely young girl of nine who was growing up quickly, and who wanted—*wanted*, mind you—to talk to me.

She was hoping I would be interested in her life, her interests, *her*!

This is the one who, even at nine, wanted me to pick her up and hold her. She would look at me, embarrassed, knowing she was really too big for this, but unwilling to outgrow it yet. She told me funny things that happened to her at school, and then laughed with the grin that is hers alone. Did I think it was funny too? That is the question she was asking me when she told me those things.

I'm ashamed to say that too often I smiled and nodded yes, when in reality I didn't pay attention to one word she said. At the moment it didn't occur to me that she was paying me the highest compliment. She was inviting me into her private world, her private world at school, of which I am a foreigner.

But she doesn't want it to be private; she wants to let me in. It won't be long before she's able to realize when I'm really listening and when I'm just pretending. My guess is that will be the day my pass into her private world is revoked.

What at times may seem like annoying distractions are really trial runs for the future. I will be very attentive when she starts showing an interest in boys, but will I still have that pass into her private world?

I will if I start looking in her eyes when she talks to me and hearing what she says. I will if she realizes that I really want to hear what she has to say. She is nine years old. In another nine years she'll be making some of the most important decisions of her life, and I'll desperately want her to seek me out. I want that private pass into her world, but I know I'll have to earn it, and I start earning it now. Perfect pearls had been spilling through my fingers, and I hadn't even noticed. Fortunately, God had.

Not long after that I sat my youngest on my lap, and, quite out of character, looked her squarely in her eyes, which were just inches from mine. I noticed how grown-up her expressions were and how often they changed as she talked. She had interrupted me in the middle of something, but I can't remember what it was. It was probably something really pressing like channel surfing or reading the paper. But I remember her face, and her momentary surprise to have Daddy drop everything and look at her so fully and completely. As she talked, I listened, and she knew it and so did I. The lights were on, but this time Daddy was home.

Things I pay the most attention to are the things I remember the longest. I have three temporary treasures right now, to enjoy for a few more short years, and there will be far more unguarded, unplanned moments with them than the other variety. I think I'm just beginning to realize that those are our real moments. It is the accumulation of these moments and their memories over time that leave the greatest impressions on us.

They are only going to be looking to see if Daddy's really home for a few more years. So I've decided to spend those years in rather than out. How about you?

> O LORD, you have searched me and you know me. You know when I sit and when I rise; you perceive my thoughts from afar. . . . How precious to me are your thoughts, O God! How vast is the sum of them! Were I to count them, they would outnumber the grains of sand. When I awake, I am still with you. (Psalm 139:1-2, 17-18)

## TAKE TIME TO REFLECT

1. How do you think you handle being distracted from a pleasant diversion by your children?
2. Do you think your spouse would agree with your assessment of how you respond to distraction? What do you think she'd say?
3. When your children are around, how attentive are you to them?
   a. very attentive
   b. attentive
   c. not very attentive
   d. not attentive at all.
4. Would you say that you give each of your children the attention he or she needs every day, or does one get more than another? How do you discern a child's real need for attention from childish boredom?
5. List what you consider to be the three greatest "distracters" in your life (i.e., TV, sports, personal physical training, computer, etc.).
6. Can you remember the last time one of your children received your undivided attention for something important to him? What was the occasion and what compelled you to give the necessary attention?
7. Do you feel you have been given permission to enter into your child's private world at school, play or work? If so, how did he communicate his desire for you to enter it? Have you ever sensed you weren't wanted in that world? If so, why?
8. Write down the three most important things you want to talk to your children about as they grow older. What plans do you have for encouraging them to share their personal world with you?

9. In order for you to become as attentive to your children as you want to be, what do you have to work on the most? When and how are you planning to go about this?

# hey, friend! could you keep an eye out for my kids?

At the time, I thought it was comical. It was certainly as funny as my friend had said it would be. Our victim didn't know what was happening, and his startled reactions to our "fun" were entertaining, the kind of entertainment young boys don't think about much.

He was sitting on a bicycle about forty feet from us. That alone was amazing to me, and it took awhile before I really believed it. You see, I didn't think at first that a blind boy could be taught to ride a bike. While he didn't ride far, there he was—our target, our victim—astride his old Stingray.

I was about eight. The boy who introduced me to this exciting adventure was a little older but clearly a veteran of past "campaigns" against this young boy on the bike. I hadn't actually wanted to join in at first, but only because I wasn't really sure he was blind. But since no adult was in sight, and it was clear the boy really couldn't see us, I soon joined in, sailing my rocks all around him, confusing him, scaring him. It was our giggling at his reactions that probably gave our position away, because he soon turned to us and pleaded, "Stop it! Please don't do that. You aren't very nice to do this to a blind person."

That plea obviously had little impact on my partner in crime. I, on the other hand, didn't like it when the victim turned and talked to me. I think I would have been happy to slink away into oblivion, but for some reason I didn't. In short, I didn't stop.

Soon our victim began to cry. He was utterly helpless and he knew it. He couldn't even engage in the human instinct of fight or flight. He was stuck. I wonder now how it would have all turned out had I been allowed to continue. But I was luckier than my older accomplice, because suddenly I felt an iron clamp of a grip on my shoulder and found myself being whirled about to face my baby-sitter's incensed husband.

> I stopped dangerous, cruel and harmful activity not because of my underdeveloped and immature moral conscience, but because someone stopped me.

I don't remember everything he said, but I remember being thoroughly ashamed of myself. One of the problems with immaturity is that we don't consider the implications of what we're doing—we simply enjoy the momentary rush of excitement and pleasure, remaining oblivious to any consequences, moral or otherwise.

Like the time a friend of mine and I were throwing rocks across the street. The problem was that we kept getting interrupted by cars as they drove past. Then, in a flash of inspiration, one of us decided on a wonderful new game. We would attempt to time our throws with the hubcaps speeding by, those shiny, inviting and oh-so-elusive targets. While it is not surprising that it took quite awhile before we were lucky enough to make contact with a hub cap, what is surprising is that with all the other clanging contact we made with hoods, doors and other car parts, no one stopped. That is, until *he* stopped.

Coming to a complete stop in the middle of the road, he got halfway out of his car and glared at us. I don't remember one word he said, but if words alone could send people into the depths of Hades, without any chance of escape, I'm convinced we'd have ended up there.

In both these cases, I stopped dangerous, cruel and harmful activity not because of my underdeveloped and immature moral conscience, but because someone stopped me. I would not have stopped myself until it had gotten way out of hand, or maybe not at all. Or worse, I would have eventually gotten bored with getting away with such small cruelties or stupidities and tried much larger ones.

In an important way these two people saved me. They didn't let me get away with doing wrong. They helped instill in my tender conscience a biblical truth—you don't get away with anything (Hebrews 4:13). God is always watching, and sooner or later your sin will find you out.

You see, there are all kinds of dangers, and physical dangers are only one of them. Perhaps a more insidious danger was the danger my character was often in. I was raised in a rural town in Northern California, and I'm not sure where I picked it up, but I had become prejudiced by the age of seven or eight.

One year, while visiting an uncle in "the city," I found myself trying to impress him and his wife with all of my "grown up"

ideas and words. So in the course of the conversation my big-
otry was revealed. The exact words I used escape me now
(thank God), but they were clearly intended to show my dis-
dain for "those people."

My uncle, who was usually quite talkative, grew quiet.
Then I heard him ask gently, "Danny, do you know any black
people?"

"No," I replied and thought it strange he would ask. The
fact was I had never even met a black person.

"Then how do you know they're so bad?" he asked. Then he
shared with me the fallacy of my ideas. I never forgot that, and
it changed me. It would probably have been much easier to say
nothing, but he sensed that my character was in grave danger.
It wasn't enough to notice this and lament the dreadful ideas
and attitudes children were developing today. He chose a more
biblical route, though it entailed more risk. "He who rebukes a
man will afterward find more favor than he who flatters with
the tongue" (Proverbs 28:23, NASB).

He did not thunder at the detestable words and ideas that
came out of my mouth because he knew I was only repeating
something I had heard. It had not yet had time to infect my
heart deeply—not yet! My uncle saw a young boy running
rapidly away from righteousness, and he intervened. The Bible tells us, "Wisdom shouts in the street, she lifts her voice in
the square" (1:20, NASB). In my case wisdom was an uncle.
A dad.

All of these events in my life are linked by one common
thread: my parents never knew any of them happened. They remained my secrets. But now I am a parent, and I find these
events instructive. In reviewing my life, especially as a father, I
have come to realize how important you are to my children. Yes,
*you*!

Though I had a good moral upbringing, my parents couldn't be everywhere at once. That attribute is God's alone. And today I rise up and call these three individuals in my life blessed. In this day and age I can't be around my children at all times. Though my wife and I have taught them Christian principles and sought to model them, I realize that their own sinful nature, combined with their immaturity, will inevitably conspire to put them in harm's way. They will be tempted to do something dangerous, dishonest or cruel. I won't always be there when that happens—but you might.

The Bible reminds us of our obligation to speak up when we see someone heading into dangerous territory. When we are told in Proverbs 27:6, "Faithful are the wounds of a friend, but deceitful are the kisses of an enemy" (NASB), we are reminded that it is easier to tell people what they want to hear rather than what they *need* to hear in order to make them, or us, feel good. Godly love entails an occasional wound as well. But it is akin to the wound of a surgeon who removes a cancer from our bodies.

The truth is that even a truly Christian home can never insulate our children from all their sinful impulses and immature desires. So I guess I'm asking for a favor, one Christian to another, one father to another. Could you keep an eye out for my kids? You can't help recognizing them—they'll be doing something dangerous or stupid, like riding their bicycles out in front of your car without watching where they are going. Or maybe it will be of a more insidious nature. Maybe it is their character and spiritual life you will see in peril. You may recognize the symptoms of cruelty, dishonesty or self-centeredness. You may see them being tempted by someone to do drugs or alcohol. You may even notice that they are playing with fire sexually. Please don't shake your head and walk away—you see, those are my kids, and I love them desperately. God put you there for a reason. Believe me, I know. God has called you and me to step in there and make a difference.

---

## Please remember that God says these young lives *are* your business!

---

One day you may see her making fun of or picking on someone smaller and weaker than she is, enjoying the temporary feeling of power. Her character is in terrible danger here. Or maybe he'll be the kid getting thrashed by a bully twice his size. You have my permission to interfere, please.

I understand that if you do this, you may get a bit of a reputation. Someone, even my kids, may tell you to mind your own business. Please remember that God says these young lives *are* your business! Jesus called us to be salt and light in our world (Matthew 5:13-14). Salt preserves; it keeps things from spoiling and going bad. Light illuminates; it keeps us from stumbling over things we are temporarily blinded to.

Our heavenly Father watches over us so very, very carefully. What I love so about my heavenly Father is that He not only watches out for and protects those who love Him, His own kids, but even the devil's kids. Even though they don't love Him, nor will they ever likely acknowledge or thank Him for it, He does it because He has a Father's heart for all. I guess that's what being a dad is all about.

So I'll make you a deal. I'll keep an eye out for your kids as you keep an eye out for mine. Was it your kids who were bullying my son and his friend? I searched till I found them and sternly told them what they had done was wrong and cowardly. They were ashamed and humiliated—and angry! Then I listened to their accusations and made my son's friend apologize for something he had done to them. I then invited them over to our house, much to my son's surprise, and gave them all sodas. We talked and laughed and got to know each other better. I won friends rather than creating enemies. Their cruelty was met with rebuke, but love made the cure more palatable.

Or maybe it was your son who was climbing on top of our street sign, just moments from falling ten feet to hard cement below. I ordered him off the sign, and he obeyed, very reluctantly. It took me months to win back his friendship for this, but your son came home that night unhurt. You're welcome. I'm glad I could be there.

When your daughter was being made fun of and reduced to tears, I stepped in and stopped it. When I saw your lovely young daughter walking out to her car in a dark parking lot, I stopped my car and waited until I knew she was safe before I drove off. She never saw me, never knew I was there. No thanks are necessary.

You see, I have an obligation, handed me by God and His three human angels who touched my young life. So in closing, I ask just one thing. Hey, friend, could you please watch out for my kids?

> Rescue those being led away to death; hold back those staggering toward slaughter. If you say, "But we knew nothing about this," does not He who weighs the heart perceive it? Does not He who guards your life know it? (Proverbs 24:11-12)

> The LORD will keep you from all harm—he will watch over your life; the LORD will watch over your coming and going both now and forevermore. (Psalm 121:7-8)

## TAKE TIME TO REFLECT

1. Can you think of some action you were involved in or attitudes you had as a child that you would be ashamed of today? If you can, share them with your group.

2. Where do you think you learned these wrong ideas?

3. Did any adult besides your own parents ever help to correct bad attitudes or stop you from doing something wrong? How did they do it? Did your parents ever know of this?

4. What do you think is the greatest danger your character was ever in? Who was the most positive influence on you at the time?

5. Have you ever had the opportunity to be a positive and even protective influence on a child or young adult other than your own? Who was it and how do you think you helped?

6. Do you think God wants us to intervene in the lives of other children we see going astray, or should we just mind our own business? How would you support your position scripturally?

7. What are the pros and cons of getting involved in someone's life in this way?

8. As you consider all the times your children will be out of your sight and possibly in danger physically, morally or spiritually, what would you like to tell those who may be around them in a pivotal moment? Write it down in a paragraph entitled "From a concerned father."

# will you be my daddy?

At our church, we always asked the church members and visitors alike to fill out an attendance form every Sunday. On the back of these we encouraged people to write prayer requests that the pastors and elders would pray for each week. I was given these every Sunday, so I was the only one who ever saw the message. It was written in a unique kind of childish Victorian scrawl that was to become so familiar to me, and it asked simply, "Will you be my daddy?"

I smiled and sighed.

It was not written by a young boy, but a sixty-two-year-old man. Balding, with a slight hitch in his walk, a large nose and glasses thicker than Coke bottle bottoms, John McCullough was a familiar fixture in our church. John was one of the best teachers our church ever had, a sermon unto himself. Rarely does one person affect so many.

I had certainly learned much from John. But maybe more importantly, John taught my children a lot of things they would never have learned any other way. John had visited our home frequently, and we had frequently gone as a family to visit him and his ninety-four-year-old mother, Gwynneth, a feisty Brit.

One important lesson my kids learned from John was the power of words to heal and to hurt. One day, while waiting in a grocery store parking lot for Annette, the kids and I were talking and laughing. Then, inadvertently, one of the children teased the others with the words, "You're so retarded!"

I could have given them a very good lecture on the power of words to hurt and the real nature of mental retardation, but I didn't. I simply turned to that child and said, "Do you think John would think that was funny? Or Gwynneth?" It got silent. Oh, didn't I mention that John McCullough, our dear friend, was mentally retarded?

My kids knew John and had wondered about his strange behavior, but at the time they didn't understand mental retardation. John had come to dinner at our house, and we had visited and sung Christmas carols to John and Gwynneth. My kids eventually understood that mental retardation means that his mental development had been arrested, and he would never mature beyond about ten or eleven years old, even though his body would show all the signs of outward maturity.

John was very functional; in fact, people were often amazed to learn he was mentally retarded. At other times it was crystal clear. He was abreast of the daily news and gregarious to a fault. He went to work every day and took very good care of his mother. He also had trouble with the simplest of tasks, could pout very effectively and drive you crazy at times.

While John had lost the endearing looks of a child, he nevertheless retained the immaturity that could challenge you and sap your energy. He demanded lots of attention, especially from me, since he had adopted me as his surrogate father. His real father, whom he loved dearly, had died when he was just a young boy. At age sixty-two, he still missed him and spoke of him frequently.

But it was my children who I believe needed John desperately. You see, their bodies were strong and healthy, their minds crisp and sharp, every one of them on the honor roll, every one of them surrounded by friends and the most optimistic future. They didn't understand permanent disability, long-term struggle, irretrievable loss. As a result, they were lacking in the compassion department. They weren't cruel by any means, but compassion is a virtue gained from depth of experience and a perspective that they did not yet have.

Life isn't easy for everyone, health isn't always distributed equally, and things they take for granted are actually wonderful blessings of God. As a dad I could lecture them till I was blue in the face, but experience is always the best teacher. God bless John McCullough. He taught my children something I couldn't, not in a lifetime. And he taught it to them in only a few short years.

> My children had been taught an invaluable lesson from someone who couldn't have completed their homework.

His familiar loud voice ringing out over everyone else's, his friendly approaches to people who were new at church and weren't sure what to do with him, his old jacket that he refused to give up, his rolled-up Levis, his belt cinched up about his belly, the perpetual cuts on his face where his ninety-four-year-old mother had cut him shaving—all the familiarities of John were not to last forever.

One day John McCullough got cancer. He went to the hospital and we visited him with our kids. John was frightened. He hated hospitals, and he was scared to death of being in pain. Imagine your ten- or eleven-year-old son getting cancer, and that was John. Our church family brought balloons and comic books and visited often. He never knew he had anything that would take his life; he just knew he wanted to go home. So we prayed, our church prayed, and our children prayed that John wouldn't feel any pain. He didn't. In a marvelous way, God spared him the terrible pain that can accompany cancer; he experienced only minor discomfort and a growing weariness.

Finally, John was allowed to go home to die. His mother was amazed at all the visitors he had. There was a continual flow through the house. I went to see him only a day before he died. He was not conscious, and I was only able to whisper good-bye to my buddy. I regretted that I wasn't able to be more of a father to him. John had wanted so much more than I could give him, yet he had never stopped reaching out to me or giving me hugs and telling me he loved me. He passed quickly. You see, John's heavenly Father loved him very much too. John had asked Jesus into his heart at a Harvest Crusade in Southern California about three years before he died. He was now in the presence of his real Father, and his heart and mind were now clear, sharp and full of joy.

At John's funeral my children saw John's friends—the friends at work that John had always talked about came, all of them mentally disabled. John, who loved a crowd, would have loved it! He was remembered fondly, with laughter and tears. My children saw all this. They are no longer afraid of mental retardation—nor are they insulated any more from pain and suffering. They realize they are blessed. They had been taught an invaluable lesson from someone who couldn't have completed their homework.

One of a father's greatest concerns for his children is character development. Unfortunately, character is developed not through the gentle winds of comfort and affluence, but through the fire of pain and suffering. I had always worried about my children in that way. I had come from a broken home; I had suffered and had sleepless nights where my entire world seemed to be falling apart—and in fact was at times. My children had never experienced any such thing.

It is difficult as a dad to try and balance our desire to protect our children from all pain and suffering with the knowledge that pain and suffering are excellent teachers. My kids have had wonderful experiences in their lives, but not of the kind that produce deep character. They have visited many beautiful national parks, amusement parks, Knott's Berry Farm, Magic Mountain, traveled to other states, received wonderful gifts, gone to great schools, lived in a nice house in a nice neighborhood and been the object of tremendous love. They have been in church since they were born and heard literally thousands of messages on God and what He wants from us.

But they have only had several moments of significant pain and loss: once when John McCullough died and another when their cousin Brian drowned. From those moments emerged depth that none of the pleasant experiences could have ever created.

The worst part is that more is on its way. My children will all suffer broken hearts, dashed hopes, ridicule, abandonment, loneliness and many other painful experiences and emotions. I wish it weren't so, but it is. Furthermore, they need to. It is only when we come to the end of ourselves that we look fully to God.

When pain comes their way, they can begin to view life from a different perspective—God's perspective. They will learn to remove their hope from this life to the next, from themselves and what they can do, to Him and what He can do. He will become their Deliverer, their Comfort, their Hope and their Healer.

One day His presence will be more important to them than ours—and then we will have done our job, through effort, tears and prayer.

Watching character be developed is a painful process. Seeing our kids suffer, cry and then watch helplessly as their dreams and hopes are dashed isn't fun. And it will happen. This world is a hard place, and while it is full of many great experiences and blessings, it will remain a hard place. They need to understand that this is not home. And frankly, I resist paying this price for my children's character growth.

When my youngest, Katie, got sick to her stomach for the first time, I was with her in the bathroom in the middle of the night. She was four or five, scared to death, and kept calling out to me, "Daddy, Daddy, I'm scared! I don't want to throw up!" I was right next to her, rubbing her back, totally helpless. I loved her so much at that moment, yet there was nothing I could do. My heart breaks for those parents who must watch their children suffer far more disabling afflictions. I wanted to cry along with her. For all the marvelous experiences that come with being a dad, this is also part of the territory.

We can't make all the pain go away and must be wise enough not to try. That is a job for their heavenly Father. This world is not meant for ultimate enjoyment or the fulfillment of all dreams and hopes. It is a temporary home, a tent at a campground. This place has been condemned and will one day be replaced with something infinitely better. We can have many wonderful experiences in this campground, but we must never mistake it for home.

One day He will make all pain go away; one day He will take them to their real home. One day they will long more for the next world than they do this one. One day, God willing, they will cry out to Him, "Will you be my Daddy?" One day His presence will be more important to them than ours—and then we will have done our job, through effort, tears and prayer.

Not long ago my oldest daughter, exasperated again by my not allowing her to go do something she wanted to, declared that I was "overprotective." If only she knew.

> And I saw a new heaven and a new earth; for the first heaven and the first earth passed away, and there is no longer any sea. And I saw the holy city, new Jeru-salem, coming down out of heaven from God, made ready as a bride adorned for her husband. And I heard a loud voice from the throne, saying, "Behold, the ta-bernacle of God is among men, and He shall dwell among them, and they shall be His people, and God Himself shall be among them, and He shall wipe away every tear from their eyes; and there shall no longer be any death; there shall no longer be any mourning, or crying, or pain; the first things have passed away." And He who sits on the throne said, "Behold, I am

making all things new." And He said, "Write, for
these words are faithful and true." (Revelation 21:1-5,
NASB)

## TAKE TIME TO REFLECT

1. Have your children ever been around someone with special physical or mental challenges? How did they respond?
2. How do you explain someone with special challenges to your children? Do you feel you explained it well enough?
3. When you catch your children saying harmful or painful things about those with special challenges, how do you respond?
4. Do you feel your children need to develop more compassion for those less fortunate than themselves? If yes, how do you plan to help them?
5. Do any of your own children have special physical, mental, emotional or social challenges? What are they, and how are they affecting your child?
6. Do you ever worry about your children's character development? What do you see is the main area of character weakness each of your children struggles with?
7. Have you ever had to watch helplessly as one of your children suffered in some way? What was it like and what did it teach you?
8. Have you seen suffering in your children produce something positive or deeper in their character? Have you seen the opposite?
9. What lessons has God taught you from your own personal suffering? Have you ever thought about sharing these lessons with your children when they are old enough?

# andrew and the bad place

everal years ago I had to sit through one of the toughest messages I've ever heard in my life. You know, the kind that hits you right between the eyes. As a pastor, I was used to dishing them out, but not taking them. I will never forget it, and it will challenge me the rest of my life.

The preacher's name was Andrew Schaeffer. No, you've never seen his picture on the back of a book jacket, and he's never spoken at any seminars in your city. (He wasn't allowed to stay up that late—he had to be to bed by 7:30.)

He's my son. He doesn't know doctrine or theology or any eloquent illustrations. He's frightfully ignorant of most of these things. He just knew that his good friend down the street didn't believe in Jesus. Andrew was only seven years old, and this thought greatly troubled him.

He'd told his friend about Jesus before, but the little boy just didn't believe in Jesus or hell. The problem was that Andrew did.

Earlier in the day, Andrew had again been trying to convince this little boy in typically blunt kid-talk that if he didn't believe in Jesus he was going to hell. Yeah, I know, it sounds a little harsh, doesn't it? I cringed when I heard him say it. (I'm sure his little friend did too.) But he hadn't yet learned how to make that message sound more palatable. He was young.

Not surprisingly, the little boy came to me complaining about Andrew. Andrew just wouldn't let up, he said. He informed me very matter-of-factly that he didn't believe in hell. I said, "I understand." He said Andrew told him if he didn't believe in Jesus he was going there. I said, "I know Andrew believes that. But the reason he's telling you that is because he sincerely doesn't want you to go there." I explained that it was because Andrew liked him so much that he was pressing the issue. We talked some more, and I promised to speak with Andrew.

Andrew was ready to talk. In fact, he was near tears. He had been praying for his little friend for some time. Climbing into my lap and staring into my eyes with the face of a little boy in fear of losing a close friend, he asked me to please make his friend believe in Jesus.

Something started to well up in my throat. After a moment I told him I couldn't—only God could do that. I told him his friend had to invite Jesus into his heart by himself.

Andrew was silent for a moment and then said, "Can I go make him run around?"

"Why?" I asked, puzzled at this strange request.

"So he'll feel his heart and know he needs Jesus in there."

Yeah, I know, it sounds silly, but somehow I couldn't bring myself to laugh. Andrew was dead serious. He sincerely didn't want his little friend to go to, as he called it, "the bad place."

We talked for a while as I tried to explain what it meant when we asked Jesus into our heart. He seemed to understand, but then he asked about heaven. He had been asking about heaven and hell a lot lately.

I asked him if he wanted me to read about it to him. He said yes. So I read about heaven to him, and some of the descriptions I'm sure he didn't understand at all, but he was hanging on every word. He was paying more attention to this than he did to the Power Rangers.

When I came to the part that says, "and nothing unclean, and no one who practices abomination and lying, shall ever come into it, but only those whose names are written in the Lamb's book of life" (Revelation 21:27, NASB), he stopped me.

"Daddy, is my name written in that book?" he asked quietly.

"Have you asked Jesus into your heart?" I asked, knowing full well that he had two years earlier.

"I think so, but could we do it again, just so I could be sure?"

"Sure, son. Close your eyes and ask Jesus to please come into your heart, forgive you of your sins and give you the gift of eternal life."

He was silent with his hands over his face for a long time. This wasn't a quick "thank You for our food" prayer. He was in dead earnest over this. When he opened his eyes, we read John 6:47 together out loud: "Truly, truly, I say to you, he who believes has eternal life" (NASB).

"Do you believe in Jesus, Andrew?"

"Yes."

"Then, son, your name is written in the Lamb's book of life right now."

"Can it ever be taken out or something?"

"No, son, not ever."

He gave a sigh of relief.

As a pastor I had been to countless evangelism programs and conferences, listened to tapes and read books about evangelism, but nothing impacted me as much as this thirty minutes with my son.

My son believed in hell. It was very real for him, and he didn't want his friend to go there. He really liked his buddy. He was willing to try anything to get him to believe. Oh, his theology was questionable at times, and his doctrine was fuzzy, but he understood just enough to know that his friend didn't have to go to hell. He knew that Jesus could save him and that his friend only had to ask for it. It all seemed so terribly simple that it frustrated him when his friend didn't respond.

I, on the other hand, was thirty-five years old, had a bachelor's in Bible, a master's in Divinity, twenty years of being born again and seven years as a pastor under my belt. My theology was crisp and sharp, my doctrinal ducks all in a row, and yet I felt something was terribly wrong with me. I realized that the thought of acquaintances going to hell didn't bother me much anymore. Oh, it bothered me mentally and spiritually, but not personally, if you know what I mean.

You see, I love the church, mankind and humanity, and proclaim boldly that the world needs Christ; but that seems so inadequate compared to my son's crying for his one young friend because he was afraid he would go to hell.

I resemble an emotionally detached physician telling a reticent patient he's going to die if he doesn't undergo radical surgery—calmly, coolly, with just the right amount of professional, aloof compassion. My son resembles that patient's father, with tears and sobs, desperately seeking to talk him into it—or force him if need be—anything to save his precious son's life. Somehow I suspect I've adopted the wrong role and my son the right one.

I recall an old Peanuts cartoon I read years ago where Linus and Charlie Brown were having one of their many deep theological discussions. Bluntly honest Linus says, "I love mankind—it's people that I hate." I fear I've become a Linus.

I believe in winning the world, training people to share their faith and starting programs. But it is my son who cries for a friend going to hell. I want to see thousands and millions of nameless, faceless people respond to the gospel all over the world. My son just wants to see one very specific little boy who lives down the street believe in Jesus, and he'll do almost anything to see that happen.

It's been a long time since I prayed for only one person—a very long time. I mean the Andrew type of prayer, not eloquent pulpit prayer for the masses that glides gracefully from the tongue and falls pleasantly on the ears, not the momentary dutiful prayer for a relative or neighbor, but the fervent, gut-wrenching, scared-to-death-my-friend-will-go-to-hell prayer. But I don't like to think about people going to hell; I find it painful. Somewhere along the way I must have stopped thinking about it, and when I did, something very precious left me. I never even noticed it.

I don't hurt as much anymore for people, but then again, I don't care as deeply anymore either. I guess that's the trade I made, and I didn't even realize it. My son showed me that it was a very bad trade, and that people go to hell or to heaven one at a time, not in thousands or millions.

This experience was still tender in my emotions when I remembered a woman who had recently moved in down the block from us. She was an older woman in deep pain, obvious and unhidden. How many times had my wife and I seen her eyes red with tears as we passed her at the mailbox?

She spoke with a heavy Spanish accent and was a very lovely and gracious woman. Her pain was from her recent divorce. We discovered that during our annual October party for the neighborhood. Her divorce had became final on Valentine's Day.

---

## My son showed me that I had made a very bad trade, and that people go to hell or to heaven one at a time, not in thousands or millions.

---

I had often thought that I ought to go speak with her, befriend her more. Although she was religious, her religion brought her no comfort or hope.

I had always experienced pangs of guilt when I thought of this woman. When she heard I was "religious," she had literally begged me to pray for her, grasping my arm gently, her eyes opening a window into the depths of her broken heart.

Before, I had been able to brush away these feelings by telling myself that I was only one man, stretched thin by the demands and needs of ministry to the many. That's what I told myself, but I didn't really believe it.

Being the veteran of countless excuse sessions I knew an excuse when I heard one, even when it came from me. I simply didn't care enough.

This wasn't the whole world—it was one woman. She wasn't too far away—she was right down the street. She wasn't resistant to the gospel—she was begging for meaningful spiritual truth and hope in her life. And she didn't need an evangelism program to meet her need—she needed one person to talk with her.

The Lord had been working in my wife's heart as well, and she suggested again that we have her over for dinner. This time, instead of resisting it (under the guise of wanting time alone with my family), I embraced it.

She came over for dinner and was so gracious and thankful for having been invited that I felt terribly ashamed that I had waited so long.

It was then that we learned what a strong family life she had in her native country and how committed she was to her family. It was this commitment that made her ache so deeply for her broken marriage. She had not wanted the divorce.

As I listened to her I was amazed again at how such a wonderful, gracious, devoutly religious woman could be so far from the simple hope of the gospel. My heart began to ache for this one woman; not the world, not the masses, but this one woman in my living room, sitting on my couch in tears. And I was touched again with the heart of Jesus. It had been a long time coming.

I shared with her the simple gospel message, including simple verses she had never heard before in all her years of religious training. "For the wages of sin is death, but the gift of God is eternal life in Christ Jesus our Lord" (Romans 6:23). "For it is by grace you have been saved, through faith—and this not from yourselves, it is the gift of God—not by works, so that no one can boast" (Ephesians 2:8-9). "He saved us, not because of righteous things we had done, but because of his mercy" (Titus 3:5). "Therefore, there is now no condemnation for those who are in Christ Jesus" (Romans 8:1).

Her eyes betrayed the fact that this was all new to her, but she was drawn to it. The concept of a personal God fascinated her. The idea that her sins could be paid for, once for all time, was strange to her. At her request I wrote the verses down for her to read in her Bible.

When she left that night I realized I had taken a small step in the right direction. What had happened wasn't a crusade or the beginning of a new program, and it wouldn't affect millions, but it would affect one person, maybe eternally. And wasn't that the way it was supposed to be, after all?

We invited her to the Bible study we held on our block. She's near the kingdom. But that isn't all. Now all of a sudden my neighbors aren't masses anymore either. All of a sudden I find I am caring for them, thinking about their eternal destiny and wondering why I haven't made better friendships with them.

## Sometimes our children see things more clearly than we do.

When our kids are little, they want to be like us when they grow up. But maybe, sometimes, we need to become more like them. Sometimes our children see things more clearly than we do. They haven't had time to master the art of hypocrisy yet, and they take things quite literally that we have spiritualized into something resembling apathy.

One of the challenging aspects of being a passionate father is passing your godly passions on to your children—but perhaps equally challenging is being willing to allow your children to impassion you. Sometimes their young, immature hearts beat more closely and more in tune with their heavenly Father's than ours. At such times pride and authority must be set aside. We must follow better examples than our own, regardless of their age. Andrew was mirroring the heart of our Lord and our heavenly Father, who doesn't want any to perish but wants all to come to Him.

In all of this, something fascinating occurred to me; there is a chance, just a chance, that I may one day grow up to be just like my son.

"Dear God, help me to grow up to be just like Andrew. Amen."

> For God so loved the world that he gave his one and only Son, that whoever believes in him shall not perish but have eternal life. (John 3:16)

## TAKE TIME TO REFLECT

1. Do you believe in a literal hell? How would you describe hell? What Scriptures might you point to?
2. Have you ever tried to explain hell to your children? What brought the subject up?
3. Have your children placed their trust in Christ alone for their salvation yet? If they have, what were the circumstances? If not, what do you think is holding them back?
4. Do you ever talk to your children about sharing their faith in Jesus (if they are Christians) with their friends? What do you tell them?
5. If your children took their cues from you in evangelism, would they share their faith:
   a. frequently
   b. regularly
   c. occasionally
   d. seldom
   e. never
6. Think back to the analogy in the book between the physician and the father both trying to convince someone he desperately needs surgery to save his life. If you applied

that analogy to evangelism, would you resemble more the doctor or the father? Why?

7. Have the actions or words of your children ever challenged you spiritually? If so, what was the situation?

8. In what way might you like to change to be more like your children? Why?

9. Is there some way in which your children's hearts are more in tune with the Lord's than your own? How has that challenged you?

CHAPTER

10

# picture, picture on the wall

They say a picture is worth a thousand words. Could it be that sometimes a picture is worth only three? If they are the right three, it is enough. Some of my most precious possessions are the pictures we have taken over the years of our children, each one a reminder of a time gone by, a time that can never be recaptured except in memory. They are gifts from our heavenly Father because they remind me of moments of love and happiness that I shared with my loved ones and friends. He not only allows us precious moments with others, but also gives us the capacity to place those memories in a vault in our hearts.

Awhile back I was going through our pictures when I came across one that triggered fond memories of our family vacations at Lake Tahoe. It is simply a picture of my oldest daughter, Christi, about five years old, standing on the wooden bridge of a tot-lot, looking down at me. She is grinning, and I can't even write about it now without the same grin breaking out on my face. At first glance it looks like so many other pictures of her, smiling at the camera.

But it's not. It is special to me alone, because it captures a moment I can never forget. We had been driving around the lake on a beautiful morning, taking in the sights, when (as usual) my young children became restless. They wanted to stop and play, not just drive around. Fortunately I soon spotted a small tot-lot, a little park designed just for our young children. It had beautiful wooden climbing structures, swings and a great wooden swaying bridge that the kids could walk across.

I let them out and they raced to the park, ooohing and aaaahing the whole way. We had similar tot-lots in Southern California, but they were always excited about discovering a new one. Soon they were scrambling all over, begging to be swung. Eventually, however, Christi, always brave and daring, had to walk across the swaying wooden bridge. Then, emboldened, she gleefully ran across it several more times. After that grew old, she looked at the distance between the bridge and the soft bark padding below. I saw that she was debating jumping. She desperately wanted to experience the thrill of flight, but it was just a little too high for her.

She looked at me tentatively.

"Go ahead! Jump, Christi! You can do it," I encouraged.

She looked at me, half-smiling, but still unconvinced.

"You can do it! Go for it, Christi!" I urged. She grinned again, her feet firmly planted on the bridge, her beautiful blue eyes a mixture of excitement and fear.

"Tell you what, Christi. You jump and I'll catch you!" I offered.

She looked at me, her blonde hair blowing softly. She was thinking about it, but . . .

I got a little closer. "Jump, pumpkin! I'll catch you, I promise!"

Smiling adventurously, she took a big breath and, tossing caution to the wind, jumped off the bridge. She sailed through the air, where I caught her and let her gently down to the ground.

"That was fun!" she laughed, then raced back up the structure and out onto the bridge again. This time there was no hesitation. She jumped again, landing safely in my arms.

I don't remember how many times she did this, and if it weren't for what happened next, I doubt I would remember much about that day or the picture. She had raced up the structure again, out onto the bridge. There she surveyed me, crouching, preparing to jump into my arms. As she did, I laughed with her at the fun we were having. Then she stopped suddenly, straightened up for a moment, looked into my eyes, smiling, and said quietly, sincerely, "Daddy, I love you."

I was startled, but managed to reply. "I love you too, honey."

Then she jumped, and we continued the routine over again, but I had been profoundly moved. My daughter had told me she loved me before, but not this way. It had always been in a natural context, in a time and place where it was expected. This was unexpected. This wasn't a "I'm going to bed now, so I'll answer Daddy's 'I love you,' with my own 'I love you.' " It came straight from her heart, spontaneously. Like the steam that builds in the teakettle until finally it finds release and whistles, her love needed to be expressed.

What made that moment so special, even after all these years, is that "I love you's" don't come easily for Christi. This moment was so special because it was not typically Christi. Don't get me wrong—she is a loving child and always has been—but outward displays of affection are difficult for her. It is easier for my younger daughter to demonstrate affection, but for Christi, those displays are awkward and uncomfortable.

This is where the dad stuff gets complicated. The problem—and it can become one if you're not careful—is that you can't always tell what Christi is feeling. When she's in trouble, her face does not naturally communicate feelings of sorrow and repentance, though she may feel it deeply. While she may feel tender toward you, you may be the last one to know about it. Getting an "I love you" from Christi is like getting service in a crowded department store near Christmas. You remain hopeful, but not expectant.

Even as she has gotten older and entered her teen years, I have to joke to get those precious three words out of her. When she leaves for school, I have taken to yelling after her, "You love me!" She half smiles, half smirks and mumbles, "Love you," as she flies out the door. I do that not to torment her or to make fun of her, but to help her. I know she loves her mother and me, and her brother and sister—she shows it in many ways. It's the words that are difficult. Sometimes she needs help with them.

I know how she feels. Some men are able to share their emotions easily; their innermost feelings flow like water downhill. God bless those men, *both* of them. But I, like most men, am not a "lovey, huggy" type of guy. So I understand Christi, and therefore I have tried to learn to make adjustments for her in this area. I make the "I love you" a fun and funny thing. But she knows I love her, and I know she loves me back.

Each child presents us with special challenges, and this was Christi's. You see, it wasn't just the missing "I love you's" that I had to deal with, but the lack, at times, of an obvious repentance when she was in trouble. Christi, I had to learn through trial and error, needed me to understand that she felt love and pain and sadness as deeply as anyone else, but kept those feelings close to her. They were private. That area of her life was not for casual public consumption. She loves to laugh, can be the life of the party, and in fact she's hard to shut up at times. But Christi's deeper emotions are private and sometimes well hidden.

This is why punishment sometimes seemed to have little effect on her. Her face would remain passive, almost seeming defiant at times. While she was indeed feeling shame and guilt, that expression simply never registered clearly. It was too easy to misread her emotions and push harder for the repentant look instead of waiting for the repentant actions, only causing her to retreat further. She was, in a word, hard to read. If you're a dad with an older child, you are probably nodding your head right now. You have a Christi.

You want something from a child that he seems unwilling to give you. The harder you push, the more he withdraws. And then you realize you are at a pivotal part of life, yours and his. Proceed with caution. You want your child to be cuddly and warm and affectionate forever. You want to be the worshiped Daddy forever. You want those days when he ran to you and jumped into your arms with his one-piece bunny sleeper on, then fell asleep on your shoulder, to last forever. They don't. They can't. And, in a way, I think it is as sad for the child as it is for the father.

Just as children outgrow the bunny sleepers, they outgrow some of their endearing childish emotions, the ones that are so very important to us. As Christi grew older, her already strong personality grew stronger as well, making it more difficult to say things like "I'm sorry," "I'm wrong," "Forgive me" or "I love you." As I learned the hard way, this can easily be mistaken for a disobedient and rebellious attitude. Now every child is disobedient and rebellious at times—it's part of our sinful nature, and Christi was no exception. But Christi wanted to obey; she tried hard to please, almost too hard. Her grades were above average. Everything she tried she seemed to be good at. Everything except being what she wasn't, and couldn't be—someone else.

---

Just as children outgrow the bunny sleepers, they outgrow some of their endearing childish emotions, the ones that are so very important to us.

---

Christi was Christi. The bunny sleepers just didn't fit anymore. Her dilemma was that she was old enough and perceptive enough to know that she disappointed Mom and Dad occasionally, and yet frustrated with the fact that she didn't know why. And Dad was disappointed because his "little girl" was growing up. It was a trying period of adjustment involving several emotional talks with Christi, trying to figure out what was "wrong" with her. I finally figured it out. Nothing. There was nothing wrong with Christi—she was being what God had made her to be.

She would never again be the cuddly, vulnerable little girl who stares at me every day on my desk in a picture. She, who in her beautiful little pink and white dress with her matching necklace and bracelet and pretty pink gloves, curled hair and pretty shoes, smiled tearfully at the camera. It was taken the day of her uncle's wedding. Christi had been so excited about being the flower girl. But now the moment was here, and it only then began to dawn on her that she must walk down the aisle alone in front of hundreds of people.

Nervously, she had come up and whispered in my ear, "Daddy, I'm scared. I don't want to do it anymore." The tears had already begun to well up in her eyes. I gave her a hug and told her, "Don't worry, honey. When you get ready to come down that aisle, Daddy will be on the other end waiting for you. You just look at Daddy the whole way." (I was performing the ceremony. Sometimes there were perks to being a pastor.)

> One of the most important parts of our Christian faith is the deep abiding conviction and truth that our heavenly Father loves us just the way we are.

She had gritted her teeth and done it. I was so proud of her. That frightened little girl with tears in her eyes standing next to Mom, looking so vulnerable, precious and cute, was captured in a rare moment. That was the daughter that every dad wants to keep forever, the vulnerable, frightened little girl that desperately needs daddy for everything. Alas, she had to grow up, and so did I.

I began to realize that though the words were hard in coming, she found many other ways to tell me she loved me. She said it in the "Drawing Your Dad" contest she entered in the paper. Her picture won the contest, and I won a cup with that picture of me on it. A prized possession. She communicated it when she always snuggled close to me on the couch, even though there was plenty of room elsewhere. She communicated it in a changed attitude she adopted after discipline. She said it in the words she wrote for me in "I Have the Best Dad" contest, and a hundred other subtle ways.

One of the most important parts of our Christian faith is the deep abiding conviction and truth that our heavenly Father loves us just the way we are. He doesn't ask us to be something else first; He loves us first, last and always unconditionally. Certainly there must be many times when He wishes we would respond differently to Him, to display our love for Him more demonstratively, but His unconditional love toward us is never dependent upon a reciprocal love from us. He's the best Dad in the world, and I'm learning that I need to be more like Him.

So you can see now why that picture is so important to me. While a picture can indeed say a thousand words, some don't have to. They may only say three words, but they are the only three that matter to a dad.

> We love because he first loved us. (1 John 4:19)

> But God demonstrates His own love toward us, in that while we were yet sinners, Christ died for us. (Romans 5:8, NASB)

## TAKE TIME TO REFLECT

1. What is your favorite picture of your children and what makes it so special to you?
2. Has your child ever expressed his or her love to you in a way that touched you deeply and you've never forgotten? What did your child say or do, and why do you think it touched you so deeply?
3. List what you feel are the unique strengths of each of your children.
4. Share what you feel is the greatest need of each of your children. How does each child differ from the others or other children in general?

5. Which of your children poses the greatest challenge to you as a father, and why? (If you have only one child, what is the greatest challenge you face in raising and guiding him or her?)

6. Regarding the child that poses the greatest challenge to you personally as a father, what do you wish you had realized earlier about your child?

7. How does each of your children (if you have more than one) communicate love to you in his or her own unique way, both verbally and nonverbally?

8. What adjustments in your fathering have you made to help and encourage each of your children? Why did you feel an adjustment was necessary? How has it helped?

9. Have you ever written a letter to each of your children, telling them why you love him or her and why he or she so special to you? Why not do that now, even if your child is very young? (You can save it and wait a few years to deliver it.)

# praying with your eyes open

t is a moment many Christian dads can identify with. It was dinnertime, and different members of our family would give thanks on different nights for our meal. It was Andrew's turn to pray; he was about four years old. We all closed our eyes and joined hands. Then he began, slowly.

"Lord, thank You for . . . the meat." Then for a moment he was silent. I thought he had stopped, so I opened my eyes. But, undaunted, he began again.

"Thank You for the 'tatoes." More silence. I grinned. I knew what was coming next. "Thank You for the peas . . ."

Andrew was praying with his eyes open, looking around the table at all the different things arrayed in front of us. This prayer would not be over quickly, especially since he was adamant about thanking God for everything, including the salt, pepper, fork, spoon and knife. Finally, when Andrew felt he had covered the bases, he said "Amen."

It has been almost ten years since Andrew and my other children prayed in that manner, and frankly, I miss it. I miss it not because of its cuteness, though it surely touched an emotional chord in my heart. I miss it because it is a good way to pray. It occurs to me that as we get older in our faith we begin to pray with our eyes closed.

It's funny—I never told Andrew to pray with his eyes open. Neither did I, or my wife, ever model it to him. It just seems to come instinctively to children, like laughing and crying. They don't have to learn how to do those things; they seem natural. So why is it so "natural" for us adults to pray with our eyes closed?

I used to enjoy his open-eyed prayers. But over time he got the idea, probably from watching others and myself, that this was "childish." So now he also prays with his eyes closed. But the worst kinds of prayers are the ones prayed with your eyes closed. Maybe not literally, but definitely spiritually.

We teach our children both consciously and unconsciously, on purpose and by accident. I am fairly certain that we teach our children more unintentionally than intentionally. While I never taught my children to pray with their eyes open, it is almost a certainty that I taught them to pray with their eyes closed, and on several different levels. We know what we *intend* to teach our children, but what are we *actually* teaching them about prayer, gratitude and life?

Living in a suburb in Southern California for thirteen years, surrounded by high-end fashion malls, the finest shops, new car dealerships and a thriving economy, we were saturated with the newer, better and more advanced. A nice inexpensive diversion was walking through one of our local malls, window shopping and spending a few dollars in a candy shop. Surrounded by shiny, new, expensive things we couldn't afford, is it any wonder that we began to find ourselves dissatisfied with our old, dull and cheap things? In retrospect, maybe those little diversions cost more than we imagined.

There were days that my son would come home almost in tears because his brand-new tennis shoes (that he had been proud and happy to get only days earlier) had been ridiculed. While they were brand new and a popular brand name, they weren't the newest, coolest (and, of course, most expensive) brand. In the cruel world of adolescent material status, he had been shot down in flames. My girls would beg to wear certain brand-name clothes from certain "acceptable" stores even if they didn't need any new clothes, because "everyone has them" (read, "everyone but us").

> What is a little harder as a dad is to ask whether I inadvertently encouraged their dissatisfaction.

It is easy to get mad at our kids for being ungrateful for what they have been given, especially when they've owned, experienced and received very nice things in their young lives, usually much nicer than we ever had. What is a little harder as a dad is to ask whether I inadvertently encouraged their dissatisfaction.

It's funny how we can honestly feel very grateful for something but not verbalize our feelings. Yet when we are dissatisfied with our situation in some way, we inevitably find a way to express it.

Although, I confess, I can be as tight as Ebeneezer Scrooge, I did find myself torn between my children's seeming ingratitude with what they had and my desire to protect them from social pariahhood. So I resorted to lecture.

I think if my kids heard one more "Well, in my day," they would have gladly sent me back to my day. I blamed Madison

Avenue and their deceitful advertising, our materialistic culture, parents who spoiled their children rotten and then sent them to school laden with everything necessary to make my child feel inadequate and, finally, the public school system which wouldn't force all kids to wear uniforms and thus solve my problem. I blamed all the traditional bad guys.

But, as you may have guessed, I never thought of blaming myself. It never occurred to me that I could have been the slightest bit responsible. I only had one pair of tennis shoes, and I wore them every day. I was grateful. Why weren't they?

Yet despite all my remonstrating, I never took into account what I was teaching by accident. For example, we have had good cars over the years, and for the most part, they were reliable. But it is amazing how old and shabby a perfectly good four- or five-year-old car can look next to a shiny new model. I was deaf to all those times I criticized my car, lamenting its inadequacy, drooling over new car ads, continually communicating my desires to have a different, better, newer car within earshot of attentive ears.

And then there was the fact that my computer was never fast enough, my house never quite big enough, my stereo underpowered, my TV screen too small, my mountain bike too heavy and on top of all that, my vacations were too short.

Ironically, it never quite occurred to me what hearing ingratitude and dissatisfaction might do to a child. It's not that I wasn't grateful for what I had: I was. But we lived around people who always seemed to have a little bit more. It was hard not to notice and harder still not to comment occasionally. But my comments were heard, and they registered.

Then, to my complete astonishment and utter surprise, my children began to be dissatisfied with what they had. Go figure. They started wanting newer, better and more stuff. They had finally learned the lesson I had taught them. My values had been transferred. The value? Around here, we only pray with our eyes closed!

## When your eyes are closed, you aren't really focused on God's provision or His goodness.

When your eyes are closed, you aren't really focused on God's provision or His goodness. What we see best with our eyes closed is what we want but don't have. Why is it that what we desire always seems to appear in our mind in vivid Technicolor, while what we have appears in dull black and white?

I enjoy taking my old childhood photos out and comparing them with pictures of my children. I can see myself so clearly in the face of my son. I know it sounds silly, but it is reassuring to me that in some small way, my children resemble me. But now I was listening to their voices, and while I discovered I could clearly hear myself in them, I wasn't comforted; I was convicted. They were becoming a chip off the ungrateful block.

But how do we untangle the inverted values we've inadvertently cultivated in our children? When we hear our children sounding materialistic, sarcastic, cruel, egotistical or unmerciful, parading our weaknesses around proudly, what do we do?

When we have unknowingly planted the seeds of our weaknesses into our children and these weaknesses found fertile soil in their sinful natures, it is easy to panic or beat ourselves up for all our mistakes, but don't. Imperfect dads are the only kind here on earth, and we can't help raising imperfect kids. It would be great if our kids were a marvelous combination of all our strengths, but, alas, they're going to be just as attracted to the lesser things of life as we are. In fact, it takes much less effort to instill bad values and morals than good ones, because their natures are just as magnetically drawn toward sin as ours are.

## We simply can't help our kids develop something in their lives that is missing from our own.

But it is not an impossible task so long as we realize that the genesis of their change begins with our own. We simply can't help our kids develop something in their lives that is missing from our own. A probing self-honesty, confession to God and a commitment to seriously address the detrimental values we may be exhibiting are the very first steps. Simply, when we begin to speak, think and act differently, we will sow different seeds into our children's hearts. When we change the radio station we hear different songs. To change what our kids hear, we need to first change the station we are tuned into.

Like eating an elephant one bite at a time, the task seems daunting, but we need to start somewhere. Besides, I want to pray with my eyes open again even if my kids don't. I am grateful for what I've been given, even if at times I lose perspective. I need to change for my own sake as much as for theirs, and I guess that's a good rule for being a dad. Sometimes we are trying to change some area of our lives in order to be a better dad, when we need to be changing in order to be a better son.

A section in a psalm of David says it best for me. "LORD, you have assigned me my portion and my cup; you have made my lot secure. The boundary lines have fallen for me in pleasant places; surely I have a delightful inheritance" (Psalm 16:5-6).

I have a loving wife, a warm and comfortable home, three healthy, happy kids, great friendships, a job I love, and I'm old and wise enough to know that no amount of money can improve on that. I want my kids to be grateful to God. They have a lot already, and I never want them to take it for granted.

I want them to learn to pray with their eyes open again— slowly, thoughtfully, considering how the boundary lines have fallen for them in pleasant places. Gratitude is a virtue that lies dormant in every soul, waiting only to be watered. It is the heart's best response to love.

If I can learn to be grateful, truly grateful, there is hope for my kids. However, even if my children choose not to follow my lead, I want them to know I love my heavenly Father with all my heart, soul and mind. Any change in my heart must be primarily out of my love for Him, only secondarily for my children's sake. I am a son of my heavenly Father first, their father second. So, whether they choose to follow my example or not . . .

"Thank You, Lord, for the meat, and the potatoes, and the rice, and . . ."

> Joyfully giving thanks to the Father, who has qualified you to share in the inheritance of the saints in the kingdom of light. (Colossians 1:11-12)

## TAKE TIME TO REFLECT

1. Have you had the opportunity yet of teaching your children how to pray? If so, what has impressed you most about their prayers?

2. Do you ever wish your prayers were more like your children's? In what way?

3. The author stated, "We teach our children both consciously and unconsciously, on purpose and by accident." What are some things you have consciously taught your children and they have learned? What might you have taught them by accident?

4. Have your children ever been embarrassed or sad that they couldn't have what some other kids have? What was it they wanted so badly?

5. How do you differentiate between what your child wants and what he needs? What rules do you try to follow in this regard?

6. Have you ever regretted not getting your children something they desperately wanted? Have you ever regretted getting them something they desperately wanted? Why?

7. Do you ever feel that you succumb to the lure of materialism in your life? If so, how do you think it has affected your children?

8. List two or three of your strengths that you feel you have instilled into your children as well as two or three weaknesses.

9. Read Psalm 16:5-6. In what way do you feel God has caused the "boundary line" to fall in "pleasant places" for you?

10. Can you think of one value, like gratitude, that your children possessed at one time, but have since abandoned? How do you plan to try to remedy this?

# failures and other deflating dad moments

It probably began when Christi, our oldest, was not more than four or five months old. Both Annette and I needed to get ready for work and school. Christi was awake and happy, so I had put her on our bed to play and coo for a while. I very carefully laid her at least two feet from the edge of the bed and placed a large, bulky towel on the side of her that was nearest the side of the bed.

I was brushing my hair when I heard a thud. Annette and I both froze for what seemed like an eternity. Then Christi began to cry.

Yep, she had fallen off the bed. I raced in and picked her up, then handed her to Annette, who, I suspect, about this time thought I was the moral equivalent of Charles Manson. Christi was fine, and survived this and a number of other Daddy failures.

Up to that moment, and perhaps even a bit longer, I had nurtured the private belief that I was going to be superdad. I would always say the right things and do the right things. I would be the father who knew best. With the extraordinary amount of love I had toward my children I could not fathom that I could ever fail them. Failure was for dads who didn't care, dads who were careless, dads who didn't have a clue, dads who weren't attending seminary, dads who hadn't attended Lamaze with their wives.

But we bring into our fathering all the weaknesses we bring to our marriages, our vocations, our ministries and our relationship to God. We wish it weren't so, but alas, it is. I believe that in a way, having kids is God's way of getting men to think more seriously about their own weaknesses. There are some things in our lives that we would not change for any reason other than a tiny little hand that clutches our finger or teary little eyes that look at us with love even when we've just done something typically masculine (read "stupid").

> I believe that in a way, having kids is God's way of getting men to think more seriously about their own weaknesses.

For example, I am a diehard University of Southern California Trojan football fan. I get excited watching football games. Quite excited. Something distinctly Jekyll and Hyde happens to me. One afternoon I was watching a close game. At one climactic point I yelled very loudly. It was a cry of total anguish, misery and disgust. It was, as my wife reminds me, a tad loud to boot.

Sitting on the couch, watching, was my youngest, Katie, only two or three years old. As soon as my scream of righteous anger died away, the anger still etched vividly on my face, I heard a mournful cry. I turned to see Katie looking at me in total fright, crying loudly. I'm only 5'8" to begin with, but at that particular moment, I felt very small. I wanted to hide under the couch with the dustballs in shame, where I rightly belonged. Katie had never heard her dad raise his voice in anger that way, ever. Not toward Mom, toward her, not even when Lady, our dog, "expressed" herself on the carpet.

Annette hugged her protectively and gave me a stern look that needed no words. I had blown it. I went over and spoke gently to her and said Daddy was sorry and I wasn't mad at her—it was all the fault of those dumb Trojans. But from that day I began to take football less seriously, and I guarantee you that only my love for Katie and my other children could cause that kind of metamorphosis in me. Failure, I have come to learn, is an excellent change agent.

There were more failures to come, far more. In our house we used to keep a stick chart. Annette and I had noticed that we were spending a lot of time criticizing our children for what they were doing wrong but very little time praising what they did right. So Annette sewed a chart with their names on it and ten little pockets after each of their names. Whenever they did something good, kind or unselfish, we called special attention to it and allowed them to put one stick in. When they had filled in all their pockets they got to get a special surprise.

Andrew had finally filled in his pockets, and I tried desperately to come up with a really cool surprise for him. Then I remembered that our kids used to love to come into our bedroom in the morning and sleep on our bed because it was so soft. One of the reasons was that Annette had bought one of those egg crate cushions to put on top of our mattress. Then I had a great idea: I would get a cushion for Andrew's bed! That sounded like such a great idea at the time. It really did.

Everything still might have gone well, except that I made the mistake of teasing Andrew about his "special surprise." I had him guessing, trying to build anticipation. Without knowing it, I was building a Mount St. Helen's anticipation in the little guy. When I finally told him he was going to get his surprise, I'm sure his little mind had envisioned a trip to Orlando, a new Honda 80 or perhaps both! When we got the little fella in his room and I patted his mattress and told him with great flourish what his special prize was, he got silent, then his eyes filled with tears. I might as well have given him a lump of coal. Dumb. Really, really dumb. The prize had become a big letdown, a demotivator of gargantuan proportions.

The ironic part is that I had only the best of intentions. My goal was to make him happy; instead I made him sad. How frustrating that is, yet how frequently that can happen! I want my kids to know how much I love them, but sometimes the way I try to show it backfires. Been there?

I want to raise children with godly character. As a result I try to encourage good values and discourage bad ones, especially lying. When Christi, my oldest, was about eight, I was told she had done something that was strictly against the rules. I took her aside and talked to her, but she vehemently denied she had done anything. That was Christi, always denying she had done anything wrong. While it pained me to do it, I had to give her several swats on the bottom and a lecture on being truthful. One problem: I quickly found out she hadn't done it after all. She *was* innocent. Dad had punished her for telling the truth. I was sure she would be warped for life.

I went to her and asked her forgiveness and she graciously gave it to me, but I could still tell that all was not right. What do you do in those moments? I prayed for wisdom. At dinner that night I looked over and saw the hurt still framed in her eyes. Then I got an idea—a good one for a change. I said, "Christi, I really did something dumb today, and I deserve a good quick kick!" She looked at me strangely.

Then I got out of my chair and bent down on my hands and knees and said, "Come on, Christi, give me a good swift kick! I deserve it!" She started to grin, but she still wasn't sure what to do. "Come on! I've got it coming! Give me a good one!" With her brother and sister egging her on, she came over and hesitantly gave me a little kick. "No, Christi, I deserve a *good* kick!" I complained. The smile got bigger—so did the kick. Of course, then the other kids just had to come over and "discipline" dad. Our relationship was restored and we had fun to boot.

This began the process of Dad having to go back and apologize for being wrong. She was very understanding—all my children were when I apologized—and they always forgave me. But I felt like the stuff that gets stuck between your toes. Since then I have felt that my dad mistakes were similar to the works of Jesus. John the apostle said at the end of his Gospel, "And there are also many other things which Jesus did, which if they were written in detail, I suppose that even the world itself would not contain the books that would be written" (John 21:25, NASB).

There was the time I promised to pick the kids up from school and forgot—and it was raining. Guess how they had to get home? There were the times I lost my temper over nothing, misdirecting my stress onto them; times I expected far more than a young child could deliver; times I punished them for immaturity rather than disobedience; and times I embarrassed them in front of their friends. My mistakes were named Legion, for they were many. Sometimes even when I was attempting a good thing, I was a terrible failure.

My son once came to me when homemade go-carts were all the rage in our neighborhood. Andrew asked me to help him build one. It was a reasonable request; at least it would have been provided I had any clue whatsoever how to do it. However, feigning confidence, I told him, "Sure, son." We did actually make a go-cart, believe it or not. With some help from another dad who did have a clue, we even managed to get the wheels to work, an improvement that was bound to make it more fun in the long run. However, I had designed the body, and it was a sight to behold. Annette begged me not to let Andrew ride on it. She needn't have worried. It soon mercifully imploded before he could get seriously hurt. My attempts at making a skateboard ramp with my son were only slightly more successful. It worked perfectly as long as you didn't use it for anything too vigorous—say, for example, skateboarding.

This probably led to the comment my son made to me one day. He had been around some other kids whose dads did real cool things like make valuable furniture with power tools they knew how to use. They could fix a car without asking their wives how to do it. They knew what all the knobs on their stereo equipment were for and how to use them. When it came to Andrew's turn to sing his father's praises all he could manage was, "All my dad does is watch old black-and-white TV shows!"

Now it is true that I am a fan of old black-and-white TV shows, and my children were the only kids in their schools who knew who Fred McMurray and Claudette Colbert were, and what shows they had starred in together. So shoot me.

But his words hurt, because they were true, and I knew it. All the things I thought I should be as a dad, all the manly things I wanted to teach him, I was hopelessly inadequate for. Andrew didn't really mean that I didn't know how to do anything at all. He had seen me at church and respected what I did every week. But he wanted to learn how to do those things I couldn't do, and he wanted me to teach him. I felt like a failure. It wasn't the first time.

> All the things I thought I should be as a dad, all the manly things I wanted to teach him, I was hopelessly inadequate for.

Having a dad who was a pastor wasn't the sort of thing a kid could brag about to the other boys. I was just a minivan dad. Those commercials making fun of dads who have to drive minivans have done their homework. Uninteresting, unsporty, unzippy and so very, very uncool to young kids— that describes a minivan, right up to the bumper! (I should know—we're on our second.) Kids are deaf to the benefits of "versatility and practicality."

Other guys' dads had interesting lives and jobs. If all dads were part of a football team, alas, I would be the field goal kicker!

But after sixteen years of being a dad, I'm still here. I'm not perfect, but I'm here. I don't know how to do a lot of cool stuff, but I know how to live, and my kids are beginning to understand that. I fail, but then I apologize, and they have learned enough to respect that. I teach people about God and having a relationship with God, and they are getting old enough to understand that maybe that is pretty cool too. Dads who know how to do all kinds of really cool things come and ask me for advice and even look up to me. They see that and it makes them think.

Not long ago I had a real breakthrough. I had to take my son in to his last day of school where we used to live. He had to get signed out. The ladies in the office got to talking with Andrew and me and asked what I did for a living. When I said I had been a pastor and now was an author and a writer, they gasped in astonishment. One excitedly told the other that I had written a book. Suddenly, from out of nowhere, my son piped up proudly, "He's written three books!"

I think I'm growing on him. Maybe I don't need to be Bob Vila the fix-it man or Neon Deion Sanders to impress my kids. Maybe the values I have spent the last twenty-five years of my life working on will be seen as important in their eyes. Maybe my dedication to God will overshadow my obvious weakness for old black-and-white TV shows.

As I think about it, how long did it take me as a baby Christian to get to really understand and respect my heavenly Dad? Everyone else's god, like sports or money or fame, seemed so much more exciting and attractive. Yet even though I didn't always understand everything my heavenly Father did or wanted, I did love Him, even imperfectly. But over time I have come to see how awesome He is.

He hasn't changed a bit, of course, but my view of Him has. I'm sure my less-than-flattering estimation of Him discouraged Him at times, and my reticence to announce my relationship to Him in certain crucial moments probably saddened Him. But He didn't try to jump through a bunch of hoops to impress me; He just let me grow up. I would change, He knew. One day I would understand.

Today I am as proud of my heavenly Father as I could possibly be, and I'm so glad He was patient through my immaturity. While He never had any foolish dad failures or inadequacies as I did, He did know what it was like to have a son who was embarrassed of Him at times. You can learn a lot from your Dad.

> As a result, we are no longer to be children, tossed here and there by waves, and carried about by every wind of doctrine, by the trickery of men, by craftiness in deceitful scheming; but speaking the truth in love, we are to grow up in all aspects into Him who is the head, even Christ. (Ephesians 4:14-15, NASB)

## TAKE TIME TO REFLECT

1. List a few of the "embarrassing dad moments" you have experienced.
2. As a new father, what were (or are) your expectations of yourself? Were they realistic? Have you exceeded or fallen short of your fathering expectations?
3. Which daddy failure was the biggest surprise to you? Why do you think you didn't see it coming?
4. "We bring into our fathering all the weaknesses we bring to our marriages, our vocations, our ministries and our relationship to God." Can you see this in your own life? What do you feel is the biggest weakness you brought into your own fathering?
5. Can you think of a weakness or bad habit in your life that you seriously addressed for the sake of your children that you might not have otherwise? What was it and what were you concerned it might do to your kids?

6. Has something your children said about you or to you ever deflated you? What did they say, and why was it so deflating?

7. Have you ever tried to do something really special for your children that they never fully appreciated? What was it? Why do you think you misgauged their reaction so badly?

8. Have you ever apologized to your children for something you said or did? What was the occasion? How did they respond to you?

9. If you have never apologized to your children, why not? Do you have plans to? What is hardest for you about this step?

10. Is there something your children want you to be able to teach them or do with them that you can't? If so, how does that make you feel?

11. What is something in your life that your children admire or are beginning to be impressed with?

# no more butterfly kisses

Few songs have been more popular in recent years than Bob Carlisle's famous "Butterfly Kisses." In his song he remembers his young daughter giving him butterfly kisses after their bedtime prayer. But slowly his little girl grows up and eventually he has to give her away to another man in marriage. Yet, as a father, Carlisle will never forget those precious memories of his little girl's butterfly kisses. The song beautifully articulates the joy, the love and the pain of watching your children grow up.

Only recently I was walking with my wife through a mall at Christmastime, doing some last-minute shopping for our kids. As we passed a toy store, I sighed. There, small children, their eyes wide with excitement, were running here and there to find the latest treasure they hoped to find under the tree in a few days. I sighed because my children are now too old for those stores. Now I do most of my Christmas shopping in clothing stores (for my girls) and electronic stores (for my son). But this was the first year that I really understood that those toy store days are gone forever. Sadly, I realize my kids are growing older much too quickly.

As dads, we say that we want our children to grow up to be happy and healthy adults. It's a lie, and we all know it. We want them to be happy and healthy children—forever. I think I speak for dads everywhere when I say I never wanted my children to outgrow their pajama sleepers. After all, pajama sleepers require little children, the kind that still want to cuddle, and kids in pajama sleepers still need to be carried to bed. Kids in pajama sleepers want to be tucked in at night and they still want you to read them a story. They fall asleep with their little heads sleeping soundly, peacefully, on your shoulder.

One of my most cherished memories is the sight in my mind's eye of my five-year-old daughter, Christi, on our first "date." I had written her a note on her napkin at lunchtime asking her to go out with Dad. When she got home she presented it to me shyly, and I told her to get ready. Excitedly, she rushed off to Mom and soon after appeared resplendent in her best Easter dress, with matching white gloves and purse, and we were off to dinner.

The look in her eyes as she stood so small and helpless and full of love, dressed in her Easter best, is something I could look at forever. That was the first of other dates I was to enjoy, not only with Christi, but Katie and Andrew as well.

I miss Katie asking me when she was three and four to watch her twirl around the living room. I would put on music and sit back as she would pirouette around the room, gracefully, happily, enthralled to have her dad watch her express herself. It always needed two or three songs before dad could get away. Now she is too old for that, and I miss it.

I miss Andrew spending hours with his Legos creating rides for his Space Theme Park, always showing them to me and asking how much I liked them. I miss watching him come down the stairs when he was two, clad only in his diapers, with one of my black pens in his hand. He had drawn all over himself and was as proud and happy as he could be. I miss catching him in the kitchen pantry with the box of vanilla wafers.

I miss carrying them to bed, all three of them, over my shoulders as I march wearily up the stairs, pretending to do it only because they begged, yet inwardly relishing every moment. I miss having them wake up with bad dreams and come tiptoeing softly into Mom and Dad's bedroom at night, whispering softly, "Daddy, I had a nightmare! Can I sleep with you and Mom?" I miss them snuggling into bed between Annette and me and feeling their fear instantly melt away and hearing their peaceful sleep within minutes. They were so frightened, so vulnerable, so dependent upon me. I was their hero, everything a man always hopes he will one day be.

I miss coming home from work and hearing "Daddy's home!" yelled out excitedly and having my knees hugged by tiny little arms and hands that love more purely and perfectly than I ever imagined. I miss waking up in the morning to my son thrusting a picture he had drawn into my face with a smile. I miss carrying my children around on my shoulders, holding them up so they can see a parade from the perfect vantage point. I miss "tickle fights" on the floor with all my children, fights that never seemed to end because no one wanted them to.

I miss watching Annette hold my tiny babies, gently caressing their cheeks and kissing their foreheads. I miss reading *Goodnight Moon* to them every night, and the Bible, *Stuart Little*, *Pinocchio* and *The Chronicles of Narnia*. I miss reading *The Wolves of Willoughby Chase* in a tent in Yosemite at night by flashlight. I miss these things and a thousand more. I miss them and I can't ever have them back. I miss telling them how much God loves them and seeing them accept it unquestioningly.

When I married Annette, I remember talking with her father at our wedding reception. I joked, "Well, now that she's gone, you've only got a few more to get rid of and you and Rosalie will have the house to yourself again."

> Through all the problems and stupid things our kids may do, there is sadness when they grow up and begin to stretch their own wings.

He laughed, smiled, but shook his head. "No, I'll miss her."

Only now do I understand what he meant. And only now do I realize what a stupid thing it was for me to tell a father, especially when I had just taken his daughter out of his home forever. Dumb. Through all the problems and stupid things our kids may do, there is sadness when they grow up and begin to stretch their own wings. We will always see our children in sleeper pajamas and remember the butterfly kisses.

I was thrilled when my children first learned to ride their bikes, but soon they were riding them further and further away. One day they won't return, and I understand that. Oh, they'll visit, but they won't stay. It won't ever be the same again, and I know it. My children used to dream of bicycles. Now they dream of cars. They used to think about going into fourth grade. Now my oldest is thinking about going away to college.

If I sound like I'm having a pity party—I am. I admit it. I feel sorry for myself because I am losing something that I relished more than I can ever say. I was Dad. I was the hero. I was the one who could always make things right, fix all the problems and save the day. Then my children began to grow up. They learned, among many other things, that Dad wasn't perfect, that he couldn't fix everything (in fact, Mom was the mechanic in the family), and that he could not always save the day. Some difficult things they had to face alone; Dad couldn't be there.

We recently moved from our home of thirteen years to a new town. One of the hardest things I ever had to do was take my children to a new school where they knew no one and leave them to an uncertain fate. Would the other children be kind to them? I remembered how hard it was to go to a new school when I was young. I remember how scary it was. And I was the one putting them through this. I had moved them. I was responsible for this pain and discomfort.

But I couldn't help them now. They were on their own. So I prayed. "God, watch over my babies. Keep them safe. Give them friends. Be gracious to them in their time of fear. Be to them what I cannot now be—their comfort and safety." And this is how it must be from now on. My children are now more frequently out of my sight than in it. Away at the store, the mall, their friends' houses, they are out of my safety zone, and there's nothing I can do about it, short of tying them down. And I don't want to do that; they must begin to move away. But I don't have to like it.

I have realized, especially as my older daughter is of dating age, that one day she will be giving her greatest love to another man, and so will my younger daughter. I understand I will one day no longer be the most important man in their lives—another will. One day my children will all marry, if they are so blessed. The great part I have had in their life will be over. I will still be important, but I will no longer be primary. I will be secondary.

> I realize, only now, that the most important
> thing I ever did in their lives was to tell
> them about Jesus, and who He is,
> a dad's most important job.

But in a way I do want them to grow up. I want them to enjoy what their mother and I have enjoyed—I want them to caress little faces and feel tiny fingers grab their own hands in total trust and love. I want them to receive butterfly kisses, and I want them to read *Goodnight Moon* to their own children and tell them the story of Jesus.

I realize, only now, that the most important thing I ever did in their lives was to tell them about Jesus, and who He is, a dad's most important job. I was able to keep them safe for many years and provide comfort and security, but I was only the warmup to the main act. My job is to help them gradually transfer their security and hope from me to Him. I have to admit to them that He is the one ultimately responsible for their creation, not their mother and I. I have to admit that they were His idea first, not ours. I have to admit to them that their heavenly Father loves them even more than I do, even as difficult as that is for me to imagine.

The best of human dads is a temp. Only their heavenly Father can finish the job and make them into what they were truly meant to be. Only He can fulfill them perfectly; only He can show them perfect love and give them perfect security. So, dads, that is our job. We have to intentionally convince our children that they need to voluntarily give Someone else a much greater love than they have given to us. We have to help them to call Someone else "Father" and mean it from the depths of their hearts. We have to do this when every part of our being wants desperately to remain the one and only daddy. It's our job. It's our calling. Until we do this last thing, we're not done.

But we'll always remember pajama sleepers and butterfly kisses. And we'll always thank God for the privilege of being their dad.

> See how great a love the Father has bestowed upon us, that we should be called children of God; and such we are. (1 John 3:1, NASB)

# TAKE TIME TO REFLECT

1. Is there a favorite song or book speaking of our relationship with our kids that touches an emotional chord in you? Why do you think it has such a powerful effect on you?

2. Have any of your children outgrown activities that you really miss? Why were these activities so special to you?

3. Do you agree or disagree with this statement: "As dads we say that we want our children to grow up to be happy and healthy adults. It's a lie, and we all know it. We want them to be happy and healthy children—forever!"? Why?

4. Every one of us has certain "cherished moments" with our kids that we can never forget, memories that make us smile whenever we think back to them. What cherished moment can you remember with each of your children?

5. Do you feel that you are, or were, your children's hero? Why or why not? What do you think made you such a hero in their eyes?

6. Have you thought yet of what it will be like to give your son or daughter away in marriage, or have him or her move away from home? If that has already occurred, what was that like?

7. Dads seem to be knights in shining armor in their young children's eyes, until one day we fall off our white chargers. Have you experienced that moment yet? What happened, and how did you handle it?

8. One of our jobs as a Christian father is to gradually transfer our children's security and hope from ourselves to God. How are you doing it? What plan do you have for doing it if you aren't already?

9. What are your prayers for your children's futures? Have you ever thought about writing one out for each of your children to give him or her some day?

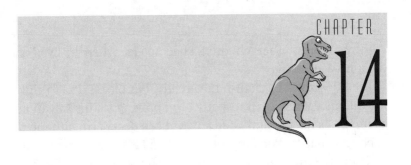

CHAPTER

14

# the father you never knew

Having sat patiently through this book, you have listened not to a unique father, but to a father much like yourself, one who wants to be passionate in his fathering. But passionate fathering isn't some new gimmick thought up in some ivory tower. It is the desire of every father who truly loves his children. A dad like you. But it is not a human concept—it is only our feeble attempt to mimic our heavenly Father's passionate love and care of us.

But if you're like me, maybe your own fathering example was less than sterling. Having little or nothing to draw upon, you wonder whether you can ever be a truly great dad like those fathers who had such great dads themselves. I pray these last few words can give you the encouragement you need to draw everything you will need as a dad from the only perfect Father.

Several years ago, I received the telephone call that my father had died. I hadn't even known he was sick, though that wasn't strange. After he divorced my mother, he had not tried to initiate any contact with us children. I had no idea where he lived or what he was doing.

The news did not disturb me greatly, but please don't think me callous. While I had recently been praying for his salvation again, Dr. Schaeffer and I had always been polite acquaintances at best. He had married my mother when I was eleven years old, and adopted my sister and me because he wanted the children in his home to have his name. There was never any great love expressed toward any of us—in fact, just the opposite at times. The five years he lived with us were some of the years I would most like to erase from memory.

To be honest, except for what happened next, the most his death probably would have engendered in my life would have been a temporary, sad nostalgia. The real blow came several days later when I received a copy of the newspaper obituary from my aunt. After a glowing tribute describing his many accomplishments in the community, it ended with a single line:

"Dr. Schaeffer is survived by his wife Betty."

Several stepsons and his natural birth children were also listed, but my sister and I, whom he had legally adopted, weren't even mentioned. Frankly, I doubt his new wife and family even knew of our existence.

Perhaps a little history is helpful. I came from three broken homes; I've had three fathers. Dr. Schaeffer was the last father to leave and never look back, continuing the pattern started earlier in my life. No father wanted me, not for long, not for good. Apparently, not for anything.

I had made my peace with this, but now, suddenly, surprisingly, I found myself getting angry. I started wondering again about my value and significance. I began to complain to God about my situation, something I seldom do. I have been blessed in so many ways that I have little to complain about and much to thank Him for. Nevertheless, this last paternal insult hurt—it was a slap in the face, one last rubbing of my nose in my insignificance.

In short, I was feeling very sorry for myself. As I had earlier in my life, I found myself again asking, "Why me? Why not someone else? Why always me?" Our memories are so short when we have been hurt. Self-pity is an all-consuming pain that has the ability to blind us to everything else in life.

> God had to remind me that I was His idea, not my mother's or father's. I wasn't an accident or simply a mistake who got lucky in life.

However, God wanted me to experience this pain because it was the only way He could show me something important, something I would never forget. Through my anger and prayer, He slowly reminded me of the words of David in Psalm 139:16: "Your eyes have seen my unformed substance; and in Your book were all written the days that were ordained for me, when as yet there was not one of them" (NASB). Every day that David was going to live had been ordained before he was ever born. This truth I had known for years, but it had never seemed overly important. Now God blazed its truth upon my heart with an intensity that overwhelmed me.

God had to remind me that I was His idea, not my mother's or father's. I wasn't an accident or simply a mistake who got lucky in life.

It's funny how we learn truths about God that sit on the mental shelves of our lives for so long, dusty and often forgotten, until one day they become the very lifeline we cling to. My heavenly Father gently reminded me that I was never an accident, however I came into being and regardless of how others viewed my significance.

I am the eternal plan of God, and there are no true orphans in the world, no illegitimate children, for God is the Father of all life. The more I thought about that, the more it made sense to me. I never chose my children. My wife and I certainly wanted children and were blessed with three great kids, but I had no control over whether they would even be born, much less what their personalities would be like, or their health, appearance or IQs.

Some of us have experienced less-than-sterling fathers. Some of us may not even know our fathers, and we feel cheated or worse—unwanted. However, God was reminding me that the best of human fathers is only a temp. However we got here and whatever we had to go through, we were *His* idea. You'll never know how much that meant to me.

All people, no matter who they are, deep down inside want to know they are wanted. There are few things more painful in life than the belief you weren't really wanted. As a pastor, I have heard horrible tales from people of how their fathers had told them they were never wanted, or in some painful way disowned them, leaving them with the same feeling.

Several years ago I read an article about a man who left his family and home to go to a chess tournament. He never returned. Ever. His family thought he fell victim to foul play and had his funeral several years later. But it turned out that the father had moved to California, stolen the identity of a dead toddler and started a new life. The truth was discovered only accidentally years later. I tried to imagine what his family and children felt when they heard after all these years that the man they had held a funeral for, cried over and mourned had never died. He had just left. He didn't want them anymore.

This is where God met me, to comfort me. "I have loved you with an everlasting love; therefore I have drawn you with lovingkindness" (Jeremiah 31:3, NASB). God needed to remind me that His love is eternal, and eternity goes in both directions—forward and backward. God not only loved me from the moment of my creation and my new birth, but even before my creation.

"God demonstrates His own love toward us, in that while we were yet sinners, Christ died for us" (Romans 5:8, NASB). Even when I didn't want Him, He wanted me. I was wanted very much by the greatest Father in the world, the one who eagerly awaits our arrival on earth and bestows a glory upon it that human sin seeks to disguise. Faith removes the disguise and we behold His love and the Father we never knew.

As I said, I was adopted. The biblical concept of adoption can be appreciated by many, but to those who have experienced earthly adoption, it holds a special place in our hearts. Dr. Schaeffer did not adopt my sister and me because I had no biological father, but because my biological father had no further interest in my life. This adoption was supposed to create in Dr. Schaeffer not only a moral, but also a legal obligation to care for me. I became a legal heir of Dr. Schaeffer.

However, human guarantees and promises are easily forgotten and legal responsibilities can be easily avoided. An adoption is supposed to bind you to someone for life, but in my case, at least, the effects of adoption lasted a total of five years, corresponding exactly to the length of his marriage to my mother.

Even at my young age, I knew he didn't love me when he adopted me. And I really don't fault him there. We were as new to him as he was to us. But how different is my heavenly Father's love for me! "Just as He chose us in Him before the foundation of the world, that we should be holy and blameless before Him. In love He predestined us to adoption as sons through Jesus Christ to Himself, according to the kind intention of His will" (Ephesians 1:4-5, NASB). Theologians are prone to focus on the adoption, but some of us find a great deal of comfort in focusing on the two words that precede the truth of adoption: in love.

"Predestined" may be a lofty concept to some and a point of theological debate to others, but to me it is a reminder that God planned to adopt me all along. Before I had ever had one father, the adoption was in the works. Not out of obligation, but love.

The cold, hard ironical facts of life are that I've had three fathers, and all of them abandoned me. I'm on my own and have been for some time. I am not mercenary, holding my breath for some surprise inheritance someday. I don't want or need it. My heavenly Father reminded me that I will one day "obtain an inheritance which is imperishable and undefiled and will not fade away, reserved in heaven for [me]" (1 Peter 1:4, NASB).

What other human father could do as much for me? So many years I had focused on my human fathers' failings while my heavenly Father attended me so faithfully.

How frail are we human fathers, so easily mistaking the needs of our children. In contrast, my heavenly Father never tires of me, never finds me an interruption or disruption to His life. My human fathers were failures at times, but to my chagrin, I am forced to confess that I too fail as a father. I can't always understand my children's deepest needs or see into their hearts to know exactly what they are feeling. At times I'm clueless.

The best of human parents struggle to understand the child who is not like him or her. I am quiet and reserved; my youngest is outgoing and gregarious. She is not adopted! I love her desperately but confess I don't always understand her. My oldest daughter is seemingly fearless, attempting things I would never have tried. I admit I don't always understand her. My son is mechanical; he understands how things work. I can't figure out the car stereo with the instruction manual in my hands.

This so often causes breeches in parent-child relationships. We struggle to love with imperfect knowledge. But not my heavenly Father. "He knows the secrets of the heart" (Psalm 44:21, NASB). "The LORD knows the thoughts of man" (94:11). No wonder God has always been such a great Dad to me. He understands me, even when I don't understand myself. He knows what I need, even when I don't.

When He relates to me, He relates to the real me, not the facade I serve up to others. But that was always the plan. Human fathers were always meant to be temporary. Part of our purpose, I believe, is to provide a contrast to our heavenly Father. The opposite of hot is cold, the opposite of up is down. The opposite of earthly is heavenly.

The opposite of rejection is love—heavenly, perfect, eternal and very, very present love.

Hey, Dad, I'm home. Thanks for leaving the light on.

## TAKE TIME TO REFLECT

1. What was your own father like?

2.  What is your fondest memory of him? Do you have any fond memories of your father or stepfather?

3.  What was the greatest contribution your father made to your life?

4.  In what way would you like to resemble your human father? How would you like to be different?

5.  In what way was your human father like your heavenly Father?

6.  What deficits in your human father has God begun to fill up in your life?

7.  What was the most encouraging thing you learned about your heavenly Father's love for you in this chapter?

8.  What part of your heavenly Father's attitude toward you would you most like to adopt and direct toward your own children?

9.  Does it make you feel better to know that you don't have to be the perfect dad? Why or why not?

10. What is the single most important adjustment you intend to make in your fathering as a result of reading this book?